The King of the DAD Jokes

By

Joe Dyson

Joe Dyson's
The King of the DAD Jokes
Copyright 2015 by Joe Dyson
ISBN 978-1-312-90407-1

The King of the DAD Jokes
is the sequel to "One Year of One Liners"

Other books by Joe Dyson
"Never Entertain During Watermelon Season"
"You And I Are Intertwined"
"One Year of One Liners"
"The Fountain of Youthfulness"
"Baseball is Full of Surprises"

Forward: How I became King

One day in August, the Huffington Post ran an article crowning me "The King of the Dad Jokes".... at least for a day. That was the morning when I discovered that one of my comedy videos had gone somewhat viral.

These videos started out in text form as a daily blog in 2007 where I wrote and uploaded a ten joke set on an internet site called "*Joe Dyson's Musings*". Every morning, I'd pump out another ten jokes and around the two-hundred and fiftieth consecutive day, I noticed another button beside the Upload Icon. I clicked it and a message asked me to enter the name of a video.

I thought, "Golly! I can actually create videos of me telling these jokes" .... followed by the realization that I could have uploaded videos the whole time. "Argh!"

So I started reciting the material in front of the camera and uploading the videos. As I approached the three-hundred and sixty fifth edition, I decided that one year was long enough. I ended the series and published all of the jokes in a book called **"One Year of One Liners"**.

I also lost my job of 17 years testing accounting software on the same day.

Finding myself with time on my hands, I decided to produce weekly videos on a new blog site called, "*The Dyson Show*". Since it had exactly the same format as the previous show, I called the first episode, "Number 366".

About a year and a half later, I was nearing the 500th episode so; once again I decided to end the series. Then, I found out about YouTube channels, so I decided to go back and film the original 250 episodes and release them all, one per day on a channel called "*DysonShow500*".

Five hundred days later it was, once again, the end of the series... however; at that point, my Youtube channel had three-thousand views and twenty-two Subscribers. I couldn't let them down, could I? Besides, the jokes kept coming to me so I kept producing videos.

Every morning, I'd log into my Owner's Page of the *DysonShow500* channel to check the statistics. "I got two more views!" was a pretty big day for me. Typically, I'd get less than ten views before I released the next week's episode.

Then, one morning I noticed that Number 504 had **over a hundred thousand views**. Having tested software for years, I knew that counters could go haywire so it didn't faze me. Then, I noticed that I had twenty thousand subscribers. Could two counters screw up at the same time? I guess it was possible.

Then, I went to the author's page of my storefront at my publisher, **Lulu.com** and clicked the Revenue button. I hadn't sold a book through my publisher in over a year.... so when the screen displayed that I had sold thirty-three copies of **"One Year of One Liners"** overnight, I knew that something good had really happened.

I retrieved my new Emails for the day and one of them directed me to the front page of The Huffington Post (UK) where the headline read, "Totally unknown comedian has over 500 videos", along with a picture of my smiling face and an option to play Number 504 of *The Dyson Show*. They had heard about me from a subscriber to Reddit.com who was one of my original twenty-two subscribers. I was proclaimed "The King of the Dad Jokes", at least for that moment in time.

By days end, Number 504 had over four hundred thousand views and I had thirty thousand subscribers.

The article sparked my fifteen minutes of fame and now you get to share in it, too. This book contains the jokes from Dyson Show Number 366 to date.

Let the jokes begin....

I called the Funeral Home yesterday and the phone rang and rang.
I guess they didn't have a live operator.

They asked me how I was doing since I stopped wearing underwear.
I said that I was holding my own.

I'm eligible for food stamps,
but why would I want to mail my groceries anywhere?

I found out something.
Don't try to take a picture of yourself with your backup camera.

I was in a 'hit and run' accident this morning.
The second I hit him, I was out of there!

During the flood, my kitchen went underwater.
My sink sunk.

They asked me how I crashed my electric powered car.
I said that I turned over a new Leaf.

They said that I kept falling down because of my shoes.
I was wearing slip-ons.

My heart burn is so bad; I've had to install a smoke detector.

The pregnant lady asked the doctor if he could perform a C-section.
He said that he'd take a stab at it.

After my physical, the doctor said that I had a pompous ass.

They asked me about my early sex life.
I said that it was hard.

To enforce the No Smoking rule at work, they posted a sign that says,
"Where there's smoke, you're fired."

I was assaulted by a band member.
He played the blunt instrument.

I looked at the calendar and realized that my days are numbered.

Big oil spills sure cause a lot of damage.... to reputations.

During a virus outbreak, they recommend that you wear a mask.
Now we know why the Lone Ranger never caught swine flu.

After four hours, even Viagra Falls.

Government officials are questioning Subway's sandwich length.
They say that the six-inch sub is normal, but the foot-longs are an exaggeration.

If they had water boarding, back in the day…
Colonel Sanders would have never kept that secret.

A dentist became a lawyer.
Then, he put everybody on retainers.

My mother had a positive attitude.
She was always positive that I was wrong.

The group tried to remain optimistic after Jim Morrison died by saying,
"When one Door closes…"

They say that Colonel Sanders was a frequent fryer.

I was so mad when they cancelled my insurance policy.
I lost my Kemper!

They asked me why I was having second thoughts.
I said because I thought twice about it.

If you agree to have your head frozen after your death,
should you smile?

I'm thinking about going back to school.
I'm trying to get into the middle class.

When I was little, they wanted me to be a Monk.
I said, "Nobody's going to make a Monk out of me!"

Marriage problems as legendary Usher has escorted his wife to the nearest Exit.

With his passing, we've discovered that Michael Jackson really *could* say goodbye.

I've upgraded my sitting position from Lotus to Excel.

To help my job search, my counselor said that I should Network,
so I sent my resume to CBS.

My Spanish teacher never understood me.

When I was little, I always dreamed of running away and joining the Family Circus.

Actor Hugh Laurie stars in a new movie about a doctor and his dog called,
"Lassie, come House"

While comparing notes, Jesus said to Michael Jackson,
"Yes, but can you Moonwalk *on water*?"

The shopping center likes to put similar stores together,
so the Optometrist's office is next door to the See's Candy store.

I got caught at one of those traffic checkpoints.
Apparently, my marriage license was expired.

My wife is living in a dream world.
She actually thinks that I'm going to find a job.

How come nobody's afraid of Witch Hazel?

As I get older, should I start using Absorbine Senior?

Her accountant advised her to do without,
so she stopped wearing a bra.

The Help Wanted add required experience with Mandarin.
I told them that I was self-taught on the guitar.

The doctor told me that I had psoriasis.
Broke my heart!

I don't know the meaning of the word, "Fear".
I should have paid more attention back in school.

I once asked an atheist if he believed in God.
He said, "Who?"

When the announcer says that the ballplayer had an abbreviated Spring Training,
did he have a "Sprg Trng"?

Legendary actor Robert Conrad is coming out of retirement to star in a western
series called, "The Old *Old* West"

I installed my satellite dish upside down.
Now I have InDirect TV.

If the coroner dies, whom do they call?

My doctor is so confused.
He says that my good cholesterol is bad.

Since I've lost my job, I've stopped referring to myself as "The Working Poor".

I'm a soloist. Everybody leaves when I sing.

I always have one of "Today's Rap Songs" playing in my head.
I walk around all day cursing to myself.

If you really want to see her face light up this Christmas,
give her a flashlight.

The Rail industry's new advertising campaign will use
a large white goose that will walk around saying, "Amtrak!"

I use my Grandmother's remedy.
I inherited her medicine cabinet.

I told my young friend that I was going to buy some typing paper.
He didn't know what I was talking about.

Regarding spreadsheets, is it possible to *Excel* at Lotus?

I lost out on a great job because I couldn't speak *ESL*.

The Beatles were known to work on writing their songs, 24, 7.
In fact, on one song, they worked 24, 8.

I got thrown out of a grocery store in Florida.
I can no longer show my face in Publix.

How to tell your spouse that you're leaving?
I can sum it up in two words: "Good bye"

How to leave your spouse on friendly terms?
Be sure to add, "Have a nice day."

I'm switching search engines from Google to Ba Ba Ba Bing.

If I'm out of work much longer,
they're going to investigate me for Income Evasion.

To appear as a real man to your kids,
Don't let your son catch you crying.

If she were alive today, would we be reading the Blog of Anne Frank?

When Superman worked around his house,
did he use Super Power Tools?

If you can't find your GPS unit,
how do you locate it?

If you don't take Viagra,
should you still call the doctor after 4 hours?

I'm the only guy I know who can fall asleep at a wake.

After the divorce episode, they renamed the program, "How I Met Your Brother."

Tonight on TV, the cast of "Bones" is chased by attackers with sticks and stones.

I needed to pump up my extra tire, but I had to wait for a "Air the Spare" Day

I had to give up fighting.
My Doctor told me to cut down on assault.

If Australia is "down under",
are we "up on top"?

My insurance man was charged with murder.
Apparently, he eliminated the middleman.

I got one of those new satellite TVs.
Now I've got to figure out how to get it into orbit.

Just after I announced my retirement,
my wife announced my comeback.

You don't want to get cut by the Fencing Team.

When they asked me how I knew about my back problem,
I said that I had a hunch.

My Mother never told me to shut up.
Instead, she told me that I had the right to remain silent.

The airport wants to do full body scans,
but where are they going to find bar codes that big?

I have to avoid getting knocked out
since my doctor told me to cut down on smelling salts.

They asked me if I ever lifted weights.
I said, "Every time I stand up."

Windows 7?
What happened to Windows 6, 5, 4, 3, 2 or 1?

You really have bad luck when your house burns down on a spare-the-air day.

Ford is introducing a new truck with attitude, called the FU150.

Little known fact: Paul Bunyan had trouble with his feet.

Hugh Laurie is considering a new TV series called, "Desperate House"

Global warming is being blamed for the shrinking popularity of Vanilla Ice.

Did they have World War I and World War II in the Third World?

I used to be a heavy smoker. Then, I lost a lot of weight.

Do Cab drivers have to pay Income Taxi?

I was counting the days until they took the census.

I went to a bar last night and got punch drunk.

I ran over my Geico agent yesterday.
That eliminated the middleman.

My GPS has a great beat.
It uses RapQuest.

You know why Pontius Pilate never caught the flu?
Because he washed his hands.

They asked me if I read that book about bananas.
I said that it didn't ap*peal* to me.

My cat is terrible at Math.
Yesterday, I caught it counting on its paws.

Michael Jackson left all of his flowers to his brother, Geranium.

After taking "Race Sensitivity" classes, I told Danica that she actually *is* a pretty
good driver.

I called my doctor and told him that I still had an erection after four hours.
He said, "Congratulations."

How do you flirt with death?
"Hi Death. Do you live around here?"

I strained my back spending money.
I over extended myself.

News from Hollywood that Simply Red is launching a comeback.
This time, he'll be known as Simply Gray.

My car got towed away last night.
Luckily I had just crashed it.

They asked the oldest man in the world to explain his longevity.
He said, "I take it, one century at a time."

There's one advantage to not having kids.
None of this debt can be passed on to *my children.*

I investigated a spot on my driveway and discovered that my car was exporting oil.

My wife and I had a close encounter yesterday.
She was coming out of the kitchen, just as I was going in.

I didn't mind having my day in court.
It was the night in jail that bothered me.

The judge asked me if I wanted a **Para**legal.
I said, "No, one attorney will be enough."

I got several quotes from my insurance agent. He said,

"To be or not to be"
"Four score and seven years ago"
"Only you can prevent forest fires"

My doctor told me not to have sex between now and next week's appointment.
I said, "There was a chance?"

The doctor told me that I had an enlarged prostate.
I said, "Yeah, I've been working out!"

It was revealed that for all those years,
Dizzy Gillespie was suffering from a concussion.

A man said to me, "Hello, Mr. Dyson."
I said, "Mr. Dyson's dead. Call me Joe."

I feel better after watching the network news shows.
I'm not suffering from any of those things they were advertising.

To increase donations, the March Of Dimes has agreed to accept other
denominations.

They asked me if I was willing to donate a part of my urinary tract.
I said, "You've got to be kidney!"

Shock in the country music world as a sex change has been performed on Freddy
Gender.

Carling Brewing Company declared discrimination today,
saying that they've been Black Labeled for years.

I once knew a Nun who had a Mother Superiority complex.

After the smog test, my car was exhausted.

In Iraq today, a car bomb killed five cars.

Before visiting a mutual friend who had a breast enhancement,
my wife told me not to say anything to make her self-conscious.
I played it safe by talking about baseball. I said, "Hey, how about them Giants?"

Initially, the inventor of the muffler wasn't sure what he had created.
He was baffled.

Hey, I found temporary employment,
I got a nose *job*.

Breast-feeding is *teat*ious work.

I was thinking of getting an implant, but I didn't want to enter the Penile System.

I remember that song, "Me and Mrs. Paul"

They asked the man why he invented the wheel.
He said, because that's just the way he rolls.

To improve my sex life, the doctor told me to only drink hard water.

It just occurred to me why Houdini never spent any time in jail.

That child actor needed some extra money, so he took out a Home Aloan.

There's going to be a new Rocky movie where he becomes a Catholic and battles the Apostles Creed.

The doctor tells me that my hair lose appears to have stopped.
He said that the recession is over.

The Utah judge asked the accused if he'd like to face a firing squad.
He said that he wouldn't stand for it.

I'm glad that I'm finally getting some recognition.
The cops tell me that I'm a person of interest.

All that working out is starting to pay off.
My doctor says that I my feet are athletic.

I don't like to take drugs for my allergies.
I'm *anti* histamine.

I read the optometrist's chart,
"One, two, three... Doc, I can't read the next number."
He said, "You have limited four sight"

They charged my doctor with malpractice, but I defended him.
I said, "Malpractice makes perfect."

Isn't a 'fixer-upper' the same thing as a 'broken-downer'?

To improve relations with the gulf coast,
BP is bringing back green stamps.

My shorthand is so bad; my spell checker actually thinks I'm writing real words.

They asked me if I gave the waiter a gratuity.
I told him that I was *gratuitful* for what he did.

I died so bad on stage last night that Geico cancelled my policy in just 15 minutes.

When asked if his marriage could be saved, Al Gore said, "Tipper over."

I realized something about my cat today.
She's a southpaw.

My zipper was down so my friend told me to adjust my privacy settings.

They asked the Impressionist if he had a lot of money.
He said that he was Rich Little.

I'm pretty sad today.
My pet peeve died.

I turned down a job at the coroner's office, creating tags to be put on toes.
I said that I didn't like to label people.

Why was there never a TV show named,
"I No Longer Love Lucy"?

If you have a question,
why can't you ask your answer machine?

They asked me if I had any single friends.
I said, "Every single one of them."

My shrink told me that I could have claimed my other personality as a co-dependent on my taxes.

When I was a kid, every time that my Father would try to beat me with his belt, his pants would fall down.

Actually, I got him in trouble once.
A guy asked, "What does your Father do?"
I said, "Beats me!"

I got some bad news. WhatsHisName told me that I have a memory problem.

The doctor told me that I'm crazy, but the voices say that I'm fine.

My boss tried to give me a pink slip,
but I told him that I didn't wear one.

I didn't go to the funeral.
I couldn't afford to pay my respects.

With my blood pressure medications, my doctor told me that using Viagra would
probably kill me.
I said, "Before or after it works?"

I tried to get a job in the Maternity Ward,
but I couldn't pass the pregnancy test.

There are three martial arts schools in my town,
but not one single "American Fist Fighting" school.

They accused me of driving under the influence.
I said, "That's ridicules. I don't even know how to drive!"

How come Ray Charles never released a version of,
"Won't See You In September"?

I was in a fender bender. Somebody hit me with their guitar.

My cycling friends asked me to join them in a Century ride,
but I told them that I didn't think I'd live that long.

They asked if my book was ghost written.
I said, "No, I'm still alive."

The bad news is that I'm living in my car.
The good news is that I'm parked in front of my old house.

I was going to buy some canned crushed tomatoes,
but I decided to buy fresh ones and let the bag boy crush them, instead.

They asked me if I had an audience with the Pope.
I said, "No, I was the only one there."

They asked me how I could fail the spelling test.
I said, "Fock if eye no"

They asked me if I'd ever been in a gay relationship.
I said, "No, they were all pretty sad."

My doctor and I agree. I said that I was constipated.
He said that I was full of it.

If toy manufacturers create dolls that are any more realistic,
we'll be able to leave our debt to them.

I almost went into horse racing,
but they're so much faster than me!

I found a way to keep the cat box clean.
Don't feed the cat.

When parking at the horse track, they asked me if I was a handicapper.
I said, "No, I don't have one of those placards.

I don't know what I'm going to do at the end.
They foreclosed my funeral home.

If the economy does a double dip,
can we get it in chocolate?

Do Catholic baseball players have to confess their errors?

My date told me that she was like the Blessed Virgin Mary.
I said, "You're pregnant already?"

To raise the morale of our country,
I suggest that we get into a war that we *can win*.

My friends told me that I walk like a girl.
I told them that it was probably the high heels.

Why does the song, "The Sound of Silence" have lyrics?

When they told me that it was American cheese,
I demanded to see its green card.

My wife is a baseball fan.
Last night, she told me, "Wait till next year."

My cat was so disappointed yesterday.
She ate the feather duster.

I have an old saying.
"The year is 1932."

My wife said that her biological clock was running,
so I asked her what time it was.

Many people don't know that the modern-day Bra was invented by Sir John Brazier.
His nickname was, "Bra".

Another early inventor, Sir John Panties invented the…

I said, "Doc, am I going to make it?"
He said, "It's up to her."

I understand that GM cars are really popular with younger drivers in China.
Their advertising campaign is, "This is not Mao's Buick".

I saw a picture of New Years Eve for 1902.
You can't believe how young Dick Clark looks.

I bought one of those new 'cross-overs'.
Now, I don't know whether I should start her up, or start *him* up.

If I get home late tonight, my wife is going to kill me,
but that's okay because I'd die for that woman.

My uncle called up and said that he was living on the street.
I got out my address book and asked him which one.

They asked me if I used a cup when I rode my bike.
I said "No. The bike has a water bottle."

I asked my mother how to handle a bully.
She said to run with them.

My answer to the doctor was that my health was in Jeopardy.
He said, "No, in Jeopardy you would answer, 'What is my health?'"

The judge said that I was going to get mine. Then he threw the book at me!
My book!

They asked me if my hotel room was plush.
I said that it had plush toilets.

I love those new self-checkout lines at the grocery store.
Now, I can smash my own eggs.

I asked the girl if I was the First.
She said that I was the First to ask if I was the First.

I got a new bed made with "Memory Foam".
It works! I keep remembering my old bed.

They said that I failed the drug test because I spelled Marijuana *correctly*.

Being out of work, I decided to 're-invent' myself.

Now, if I could just figure out *what* I've invented.

My doctor said. "I have bad news. You only have six months to live."
I said, "Thank God! I thought you were going to tell me to stop smoking."

My wife is so emotional. I told her that I'd never leave her. Never!
She started to cry.

To stop my video addiction, the doctor tied my Youtubes.

She said that she wouldn't sleep with me on the first date.
I told her that I would try to stay awake, too.

I got a sign from God last night.
I backed over it in the church parking lot.

I tried to open an Indian casino,
but I didn't have a reservation.

We're not supposed to honor false Gods.
I hate True/False questions.

You know that it's going to be a long trial if the judge says,
"Jehovah, call your first witness."

I notice that the dog pound never tells you how many pounds of dogs they have.

I heard that you could lower your cholesterol by taking Crestor.
Hey, I've been brushing my teeth with that stuff for years! Crestor…

I finally met a woman with Class.
She's a schoolteacher.

One of my old friends found me on Facebook.
Apparently, I owed him some money.

I'm trying to use less energy,
so I gave up those energy drinks.

My car has seventy-five horsepower,
with makes it more powerful than my seventy-four horses.

Why doesn't anybody pray to St. Petersburg?

I got some bad news today.
My publisher wants to remove my appendix.

I got bad news today.
My Doctor told me to cut down on eye candy.

My car is a chick magnet.
I've hit three of them so far.

When my dog sat up, rolled over and begged,
I said, "Oh, up to your old tricks, huh?"

My wife told me to act my age,
so I'm using the term, "By Cracky" a little more.

Another attack by the "Underwear Bomber".
He blew up a three-pack.

They asked me how I've been married for so long.
I said that I take it, one woman at a time.

The interviewer asked what my driving force was.
I told him that I had a Toyota.

With all this talk about 'jump-starting' the economy,
why don't they just call Triple-A?

The store said that the restrooms were for employees only.
So I applied for a job.

I applied for a position of an "Early Educator",
but, apparently getting up at Six AM wasn't good enough for them.

When my father said that he didn't have a sense of humor,
he wasn't kidding.

It always bothers me when I go in for a physical,
and the doctor is surprised to see me.

I put one of those alarms on my car.
Now, the horn blows while *they* drive it away.

Every time they asked the defendant about the liquor store robbery,
he took the fifth.

The Interviewer asked me if I was drug free.
I said, "No, they're pretty expensive."

Tiger announced that he didn't have an estranged wife.
He had Curtis Strange's wife.

After posting quarterly loses,
Proctor immediately blamed Gamble.

I tried to book a flight using Orbitz.
You know that you have to go all the way around with Orbitz!

I asked the doctor if I should get laser eye surgery.
He looked right through me!

If you're looking for work on Craigslist,
don't look under, "Men seeking men".

The Doctor told me to take the medicine before the expiration date.
I didn't realize that he meant, *my* expiration date.

They asked me if I wanted to be a living donor.
I said that I'd rather donate *after* I died.

I've discovered that my comedy career is not a laughing matter.

There are people who think that the world is going to end next year.
Great! Just when the Recession is over!

How come, during a hunger strike, nobody ever chants,
"Hell no, we won't eat!"

Hey, I found out that I might get on TV.
Dog the Bounty Hunter is looking for me.

When my wife told me that there was another man,
the first thing I said was, "Does he have a job?"

How can you tell a zebra from a horse that busted out of jail?

Great news at my old job.
I was named Former Employee of the Month.

A, E, I, O, U and sometimes Y.
I just had a vowel movement.

I was thinking of getting a mobile phone,
so I can call up my car. (Hey, where are you?)

I've cut my golf score in half.
I'm only playing nine holes nowadays.

How about the custom of giving people nicknames based on their looks, like Shorty.
What would you call a short, fat, red haired, left-handed guy?

You hear about all these people coming out of the closet,
but you never see them, blinking to the light.

In order to write her life story,
they took a book right out of Patti's Paige.

New software comes with a Readme file.
Why don't new cell phones come with a Callme file?

I was feeling Frisky last night until my cat tried to eat me.

They asked if my wife was true to me.
I said, "Only when she's under oath."

My former company finally posted a profit.
It was in the amount of my former salary.

It was reported that singer; *Dusty* Springfield was not a very good housecleaner.

I bought that new speech recognition software.
Now, my computer understands it when I call it a piece of shit.

Remember 1968 VW Vans? They're being recalled for accelerators problems.
It's been reported that they can, suddenly accelerate up to 35 mph!

My cat got bad news today.
Her vet got sick, so they put him to sleep.

You know why former President Bush never goes outside anymore?
Because he doesn't have an exit strategy.

I felt like a superhero on the day that laid me off.
I said, "My job here is finished"

I wanted an A-Frame House, but I didn't want a large A-Frame,
so they built it in lower-case.

Instead of calling capital punishment, "Executions",
they're going to call it, "De-Friending".

Obesity is a huge problem!
… Big problem…
… Large problem…

I almost got a chance to entertain at San Quentin,
but they found me, Not Guilty.

My wife said that she was going to take Karate lessons.
I said, "Okay! I *will* do the dishes!"

To break my addiction to soul music,
my doctor told me to give up Smokey.

Times have sure changed.
Now, it's the employers telling the *employees* to take this job and shove it.

The bully said that he was going to beat me within an inch of my life.
I said, "Oh yeah? Let me go get a ruler."

I got bit by a dog yesterday.
I said to the blind guy, "Did you see that?"

I never had trouble talking to my parents.
I was always saying, "I'm telling Mom!"

They said that the legal limit for drinking is "Point Eight".
I said, "Man, that's pretty young."

Everybody always remembers the good old days.
Why doesn't anybody remember the good old nights?

When the movie was over,
why didn't they call it a "Drive-out theatre"?

The girl asked me why I stood her up.
I said because the bar was closing.

It seems like yesterday when my father finally talked to me about sex.
I said, "Dad, you are aware that I'm 58, right?"

I have a great dentist.
He can clean my teeth and my wallet at the same time.

If the pregnancy test comes out positive,
did your teenage daughter pass it or fail it?

They don't have dog racing in California.
The mailman just gives up and stands there.

I asked the contractor if there was a future in home building.
He said that the roof was the limit.

18

They asked me if I still said my prayers.
I said, every time I ride in a taxi.

It's great to live in liberal California!
My wife was going to kill me for being late
but a group of protesters picketed the house.

When my cardiologist said that I might be having an arrest,
I chanted, "Attica! Attica!"

Ever since I took the mirror off my car,
I've never looked back.

Why does it take Dog the Bounty Hunter a full hour to catch somebody?

Nowadays, everybody thinks that I have a cell phone,
just because I walk down the street talking to myself.

They asked Batman why his partner was named, "Robin".
He said because it sounded better than "Batman and Dick".

One day my Father said to me, "You're in trouble!"
I said, "I'm pregnant?"

They asked me if I wanted to drag race.
I said, "Sure, as long as I can dress like a man."

Hey, I might get on TV!
If I lose my house, I'll be on The Streets of San Francisco.

I had to take the doorbell off my house to get Avon to stop calling.

I was quiet last night so my wife said, "Cat got your tongue?"
I had to signal the cat to say, "Yes"

I know a singer who became an English teacher.
Her class was called, "Peaches and Verbs"

My singing is so bad that all of my friends have cancelled their birthdays.

They asked me if I had any gay friends.
I said, "Is Tom Shane gay?"

Wouldn't the Lethal Injection drug's expiration date
be the same date that it was administrated?

Every job that I see listed seems to require a drug test.
I don't know anything about drugs! How can I pass it?"

I think the doctor was reading the wrong chart when he said,
"Mr. Dyson, your wife had a baby girl."
I said, "But she's in her mid fifties!"
He said, "Well, it's an old baby girl."

Why are there so many doctors named "Umentary"?
It seems like every town has a Doc Umentary

Do you know what I really missed about the last decade?
Sergio Mendes and Brazil 06.

How come State Farm doesn't grow anything?

During the football game at the two minute warning,
how come nobody runs around yelling, "Warning! Warning!"

The insurance company says that I can save fifteen percent in just fifteen minutes.
Well, what if I talk to the guy for a hundred minutes?

I told the lady that I used body language.
She said that I had bad diction.

I appreciated the doctor asking if I had insurance,
until I realized that he meant, *Life* Insurance.

You know the problem with lying on your resume?
Everybody thinks that you're over qualified.

I've been having bad dreams recently.
The acting has been terrible, and the plots! Oh brother!
Who writes these things?

The new ATM machine at my bank doesn't require deposit slips anymore.
How did they know that I was unemployed?

The critic said that he didn't like my style of comedy.
I said, "I have style? Thank you!"

I'll always remember my first car.
I'm living in it.

I bought one of those car alarms.
Now, it wakes me up when I get to work.

An apple a day keeps the doctor away.
Adam and Eve sure wished that God were a doctor!

My agent hasn't gotten me into a single nightclub,
but he's gotten me lots of insurance.

It sure is tough getting older.
Every time I see a pretty girl,
she's young enough to be *your* daughter.

Do you realize that our children today will never be able to say,
"Back in the good old days"?

They asked me why my book doesn't have a Table of Contents.
I said because I was selling it, unfurnished.

I knew that there might be a layoff at work when the sign in the employee kitchen said,
"Your mother doesn't work here, and neither do you."

My wife complains about my spending.
She's always saying, "Spend some money! Buy something! Underwear! Anything!"

More bad news for the auto industry.
I laid off my car yesterday.

They're making a new movie about McDonalds.
It's called, "Waiting for Super size."

The doctor put me on a cholesterol medicine.
I said, "Doc, this drug is so expensive, I won't be able to afford to eat."
So he put me on a diet, too.

The job interviewer said that he had zero tolerance for drugs.
I said, "Do you have better luck holding your liquor?"

A new Rocky movie is coming out where he goes back in time, and battles Apollo 7.

My accountant asked me if I depreciated my car.
I said, "Every time I start it up."

The doctor told me to cut down on salt,
so I canceled my vacation to the Great Salt Lake.

They asked me what time I was born.

Well, being so young at the time, all I could say was, "The big hand was on the 6 and the…"

They advise calling your doctor if Cialis causes vision loss,
But they don't tell you how to find your phone.

They asked me what I thought about short skirts.
I said that they make my knees look boney.

Wouldn't it stand to reason that, if they don't sentence you to death, they sentence you to life?

They said that everybody was sick of my jokes.
I said, "Well, thank goodness for universal health care!"

Sports programs have so many commercials for Cialis
that I feel like I should smoke a cigarette afterwards.

They said that I don't believe anything that anybody tells me.
I said, "Really?" "Really?"

The job interviewer asked if I could handle heavy phones.
I said, "As long as they're not over fifty pounds."

A guy asked me if I believe in "Don't ask, Don't tell".
I said, "Don't ask"

They asked me how many bars my phone has.
I said that I've left my phone in six bars so far.

I found out the hard way that it was deer hunting season.
There was gunfire in my neighborhood,
so I sent my deer out to investigate.

Can you write a new chapter to your life if you've already written the epilog?

They asked me if I wanted to take rapid transit.
I said, "I hate to make quick decisions"

I notice that you get right through airport security if you take Naked Airlines.

To increase ratings, CBS is renaming the show,
"Facebook the Nation"

When he was given the Ten Commandments on the heavy stone tablet,
Moses asked, "Do you have a Kindle version of this?"

I told the guy that my wife burned our dinner last night.
He asked me how bad?
I said, "Three alarms."

If they repeal the health care bill,
do I have to give back the six months that the doctor gave me?

My canary is into computers.
This morning she tweeted me.

I was going to write my own obituary,
but then, it would be Ghost written.

I wanted to end a magazine subscription but they redirected me to a suicide hotline.
That's what happens when you try to cancel Life.

I told the doctor that I had to get up every two hours.
He said, "To go to the bathroom?"
I said, "No, to move my car."

I had to change the brand of oil that I use.
My doctor told me to cut down on sweet crude.

After the oil spill in the Gulf,
the EPA says that the fish are getting much better mileage.

They asked me what I bought with my disposable income.
I said, "Disposable razors"

The best part about having a home office,
is that it's close to the employee kitchen.

Who do you call if your car is stolen by the On-Star operator?

Hey, my wife got us on TV!
Tonight, we're going to be on Divorce Court.

They asked me what it was like to drive over the Golden Gate Bridge every day.
I said that it took a Toll on me (six bucks!)

They asked me if I could juggle.
I said, "Look! I only have two hands!"

They told me that I only had a week to live.
I said, "Okay, but I'm not working any overtime!"

If they were written today,

would we be reading the Dead Sea Blogs?

The guy with the gun said that he was going to *take me out.*
I said, "Oh yeah? What time are you going to pick me up?"

If our president dropped a bomb somewhere,
would it go O**BOOM**A!

My parents thought that I had amnesia.
They were always saying, "Who do you think you are?"

The accelerator stuck on my car and it was terrible!
I got to work twenty minutes early!

The lady said that I was half the man that her husband was.
I said, "Your husband is eleven feet tall and three hundred pounds?"

I told my wife that nobody at work takes me seriously.
She said, "Why don't you do your comedy act for them?"

The doctor told me to live for Today.
I told him that I'd rather live for Good Morning America.

They asked me if I was a finicky eater.
I said, as long as the finicky is vegetarian.

I got bad news today.
I found out that my Family Tree has termites.

When they invented the typewriter, did somebody say,
"This is the next best thing since handwriting?"

The doctor tapped me on the knee and I belched.
He said that my acid reflexes were fine.

I was so disappointed with my new electric vehicle.
They won't let me take it off the golf course!

When the doctor said that I owed him a lot of money,
I said that I was in denial.

They asked me if I could teach Drivers Ed.
I said, "As long as Ed listens and follows directions"

I'm initiating a new policy:
"I didn't ask, please stop telling me."

When asked why he moved from a continent to an island,
he said that he was tired of being incontinent.

Many married women today do not use their husband's last name.
In fact, Kenny G's wife uses her maiden initial.

Years ago, there was a song by Bobby Goldsboro. You know the one I mean.
In that song, was he singing about Honey Goldsboro?

They used to have an old saying down in Hollywood:
"Only you can prevent Forrest Tucker"

While reporting the holdup, they asked me if it was a hate crime.
I said, "No, he seemed to enjoy crime."

The military is starting a new policy called,
"Don't ask, wait for WikiLeaks to tell us"

They asked me when I last saw the deceased.
I said, "When he was alive"

The only problem I've had with driving while talking on the phone,
is when I start to pace.

After she died, how come they never made a show called,
"The Ghost *Is* Mrs. Muir"

I asked my doctor why he filmed all of my appointments.
He said, because he's not a real doctor. He just plays one on TV.

You think that WikiLeaks are bad,
wait until they start taking WikiDumps!

I said, "Chute didn't open!"
He said, "Don't you mean, 'the **para**chute didn't open'?"
I said that I was **para**phrasing.

My car has one of those new backup cameras.
Do you know how hard it was to take all those wedding pictures in Reverse?

I told the officer I could prove that I hadn't been drinking.
I had just come from a no-host bar.

They asked me what color my car was.
I said, "Prematurely gray."

I don't know why they don't let you text and drive.

I mean, I can drive with two fingers!

I asked my friend if he was gay,
but he wouldn't give me a straight answer.

I tried but I couldn't act like a Republican.
My bleeding heart wasn't into it.

To balance my budget, I'm making some painful cutbacks.
I'm not buying aspirin any more.

NPR wants to become more conservative,
so they're creating a new program called,
"No Things Considered"

I just realized that to take advantage of the Bush era tax cuts,
I'm going to have to get a job!

When the cops use Pepper Spray,
how come nobody sneezes?

During the trial, a lady went into labor.
The Judge delivered the baby by sentencing it to life.

I realized today, that I don't know anything about the back of my hand.

How come Cher never put out a version of,
"Don't Let Sonny Catch You Crying"

Why is Canada Dry, wet?

They asked me if I practiced my religion.
I said, "No, I just go down there on Sunday and wing it."

I cancelled my camping trip,
because I couldn't wake up my sleeping bag.

They asked me if I practiced safe sex.
I said, "Yes, I use a net."

I think that my dentist is using his own laughing gas.
You should have heard him when he handed me the bill.

OJ tried to break out of prison this morning,
however an official caught him jumping off sides.

I told my friend that I got lucky last night.

26

He said, "You found a girl?"
I said, "No, no! Not THAT lucky. I won the lottery."

You know what I found out today?
You don't have to be 21 to go into a salad bar.

The bartender told me that I was over the limit.
I said, "Buddy, I'm only five foot six."

If you live in a mobile home,
can your foreclosure be repossessed?

To help out with the war effort,
the president wants to send the Commodores over there.

The doctor said that I might not make it through Tonight.
I said, "How about if I watch Late Night instead?"

Regarding folk singers,
am I the only one that thinks The Smothers Brothers are
Tom, Dick and Mary?

There are no guarantees in life,
which is why I bought an extended warranty.

The doctor said that I had 24 hours to live.
I said, "Starting when?"

They're going to release an updated version of the movie, "Rearview Mirror".
The new film will be called "Backup Camera".

I had a Falcon once,
but it flew away.
I had a T-Bird once,
but I traded it for the Falcon.

I asked a truck driver if he was a pro.
He said that he was Semi-pro.

You know one thing that I've never done in my life?
Marched into hell for a heavenly cause.

There are doctors today who do not carry around small change.
They're known as "Doctors Without Quarters".

I only had time for a two-hour date,
so I only took half of a Viagra.

I can't play Smokey Robinson songs on Spare the Air Days.

I was told that if I took up the drums,
there would be repercussions.

They asked me why I moved to The West Coast.
I said because of the West Coast Offense.

I got bad news from my vet today.
He said that my Party Animal died.

What type of car is the military using
to drive out the Taliban?

They asked me if I wanted a hunting dog.
I said that I was a vegetarian. I don't hunt dog.

I wanted to watch "NFL Today", but I have a really old TV,
so I had to watch "NFL Three Weeks Ago"

Since I started volunteering at the Food Bank,
I'm not hungry anymore.

They asked me if I ever streaked.
I said, "Back when I had enough hair."

My dentist wants me to practice *preventative hygiene.*
Wouldn't I be preventing hygiene if I just stopped bathing?

If Chevy Chase named a son after himself,
would the kid be Chevy II?

I have always worked my butt off!
However, since I've lost my job, it's starting to grow back.

In the history of pharmaceuticals, those little pills got their start in Great Britain.
They were known as Carter's Little LiverPools.

One of the hardest parts about having a hyphenated name is when you have to spell
it out:
H-Y-P-H-E-N...

You know which celebrity should have been an organ donor?
LIVERace

He said that he was going to beat the daylights out of me.

28

I said, "Why don't we save some time and do it at night?"

I had a co-worker ask me if I wanted to hit the bar after work.
We spent the evening doing chin-ups.

You know, every time I reply to a job offer on Craigslist,
I get an immediate email response saying that they've already hired Craig.

They asked me if I knew the way to San Jose.
I said, "No, but I do a great rendition of 'Walk On By'"

They asked me when I became a pacifist.
I said when I got into my first fight.

My co-worker asked me if I wanted to hit the gym.
I said, sure, so we beat up Jim

To build up my confidence, my psychiatrist suggested that I dream the *possible* dream.

As a child, my parents told me that should get a college degree.
And they were right!
I needed my college degree to get the job that I was laid off from.

Katie Couric was asked if hosting the CBS evening news had changed her.
She said, "No, and for more on this, here's Nancy Cortis in Washington…"

The caller asked if I ever used the 'redial' feature on my phone.
I hung up, called him back and said, "Yes."

They asked me what my taste in music was.
I said that I ate rock and roll.

They asked me if I was into hip-hop.
I said, "Not since my horse ran away."

I can't believe it! My doctor gave me a prescription for the lethal injection drug.
… but it only has one refill!

In the sawmill accident, the man lost his right arm.
He only had one left.

They asked if my parents always had custody over me.
I said that they were always cussing over me.

I got bad news from my dentist today.
He said that I was long of tooth.

Can you take your car to Aamco if the horn doesn't blow?
"Double A…, Double A……"

I asked the man why he visited the funeral home every afternoon.
He said that he was living each day as if it were his last.

I didn't know where I was going on vacation,
so I bought one of those GPS units.
Now, IT doesn't know where we're going.

When I complained to the doctor about fatigue,
he suggested that I stop wearing the Army uniform.

I got my first paycheck from my new job at the local Food Bank.
When I cashed it, all they gave me was food.
I should have gotten a job at a Money Bank!

Now that NPR may lose their federal funding,
they're going to start a new drive called, "Pledge Year"

I saw a job offer for an un-armed security guard.
How's he supposed to pull his gun?

They asked me when I used my Occasional Table.
I said that I used it more than my Never Table.

I told my wife that nobody takes me seriously.
She said, "Are you serious?"

I got bad financial news yesterday.
My living trust died.

They asked me when I last saw the deceased.
I said, "Back at the Funeral Home."

I was born on such a poor side of town,
my next-door neighbor was Johnny Rivers.

Some people say that Jesus was a prophet,
however the church says that He was Not-for-Profit.

They asked me if I was aware that "Tsunami" is spelled with a silent "T".
I said, "I know with a silent "K""

Actually, "Tsunami" is the new word for what we used to call, "Sidal Wave"

My grandfather can't die.
He lives in a No Passing Zone.

I asked the doctor what my options were for the bags under my eyes.
He said, "Paper or plastic."

My friend told me that they don't bathe anymore.
I said, "I know. I got a whiff of your wife."

They're going to create a remake of Bing Crosby's movie, only this time, he
doesn't become a priest. It will be called, "Not Going My Way"

I stopped eating Jell-O when I found out that it was made out of horse's hooves.
Hey! I know what they step in!

How come The Mamas and Papas never had any children?

If somebody says, "I can't thank you enough,"
shouldn't you reply, "And I can't say 'you're welcome' enough"

They suspected that the cop had started drinking again,
when he fell off the paddy wagon.

I don't have to mow my lawn anymore.
I told my neighbors that the state flower was grass.

They say that Johnny Cash almost named his famous song,
"A Boy Named Rosanne"

I was watching the Sugar Bowl last winter
when a neighbor came over and borrowed a cup of it.

When the doctor told Patrick Henry that he was going to die,
he said, "Give me liberty instead"

My dog used to be under voice control,
until I lost my voice yelling at it.

I'm so depressed.
My virgin olive oil got pregnant.
…And it was extra virgin, too!

Funding was cut in half to the March of Dimes.
They will now be known as the March of Nickels.

I can't remember if I've ever had amnesia.

I asked my uncle if he ever mixed music and drugs.
He said that he used to smoke Teddy PenderGrass.

They asked me if I wanted Tommy John surgery.
I said that my insurance wouldn't cover him.

They asked me if I ever saw a waterspout.
I said, "Yes, at least three times every night."

I remember telling my Army recruiter,
"I want to go to Iraq! I want to go to Afghanistan!"
He said, "But it's 1970 and we're fighting in Viet Nam."
I said, "I know."

My friend asked me if his wife was having an affair.
I said that I keep out of other people's affairs.

They told me that Kragen Auto Parts is changing their name to O'Reilly.
I said, "Oh Really?"

Legendary Phil Specter attempted to break out of jail last night.
They caught him trying to go over the wall of sound.

My doctor told me to cut down on salt and pepper,
so I'm going to dye my hair.

Never ask a cannibal who he's having for dinner

It doesn't matter what flavor cat food I buy, they all taste like chicken.

In the Soviet Union, is their cable company called, "CommieCast"?

You'd think that my wife owned a football team.
She's imposing a lockout on me.

They asked me how I was going to get my car out of the driveway.
I said that I had a backup plan.
I call it, "Plan R"

I advised the crook that he shouldn't rob me because I didn't have any money….
So he took my advice.

They asked me if I used a hand-held device.
I said, "Only when I'm at the urinal."

Do chiropractors have to pay *Back* taxes?

My health is so bad that my doctor suggested that I give up living.

My tax preparer asked me how I earned so much money under the table.
I said, "Because I'm a table repairman."

They asked me what my score was on the drug test.
I said, "420"

My doctor won't discuss things with me. I asked him how to lower my cholesterol and he told me to shut my pie hole.

If your house floods, and you owe more than it's worth,
Is it under *under* water?

They say that the oceans could rise up to one meter by the next century,
but I doubt if they'll rise more than 39.37 inches.

One advantage to getting older is that there are fewer elders to show respect for.

The members of the rock group, "Three Dog Night" are so old that they put out a song called,
"Hard to be Hard"

I wanted to raise my debt ceiling, but I couldn't reach it.

They asked me why I don't spend my money at the bar anymore.
I said that I was in economic recovery.

If the price of cigarettes goes up any higher,
I won't be able to afford to die.

I always thought that Ted Nugent was that stuff inside the Three Musketeers bar.

They asked Tony Orlando if he ever had an affair with his backup singers.
He said that it never Dawned on him.

People always take me so seriously.
I mean, do you really believe that two guys came walking into a bar?

My doctor told me to stop eating French Fries.
There goes my trip to France!

Why does Ford say such bad things about their own full sized pickup truck?
I mean, they're always saying "**F 150! F 150!**"

There's a new radio station that features,
"Light rap, less cussing"

I asked my friend if it was different being in a same-sex marriage.
He said, "No, it's the same."

After getting laser eye surgery, my friend said that he can see Twenty-Ten.
I said, "Gee, it's too bad that it's Twenty-Fifteen."

After reading my book, they said that I had sold out.
I said, "No, I've still got hundreds of copies out in my garage."

Last Saturday, I went into the church confessional and said,
"Bless me, Father for I have sneezed"

They asked me what I majored in back in college.
I said, "Procrastination"
They asked me if I graduated.
I said, "Aaaa, not yet."

I had a conversation with my garbage man this morning.
We were trash talking.

I told my doctor that I felt down in the dumps.
He told me to start recycling

With so many banks being taken over by the Feds,
our local Food Bank has been taken over by the Un-Fed.

If you choose to leave your gun at home,
are you un-packing?

They asked me why I was rubbing my wrinkles.
I said that I was feeling my old self.

It sure is depressing having to vote the bums out,
just four years after voting them in.

It's amazing what you can find out on the Internet.
I Googled myself and discovered that I invented the vacuum cleaner.

I'm so depressed.
Tom Shane un-friended me.

They found an un-released song in the vault of Michael Jackson called,
"I Lied, Billie Jean WAS My Lover"

The space shuttles were retired because their computers were still running on DOS.
Apparently you can't have a space ship without Windows.

34

I'm taking advantage of this new 'Anti-Bullying' campaign.
So far, I've gone up to every bully I know,
slapped him around a few times and took his lunch money.

The chef was serving kurds and whey.
I wanted one but not the other, so I said,
"Kurds, no whey"

They asked me why I always talk so loud.
We said, "Because we're always talking in the third person"

Many people smoke a cigarette at seven o'clock.
That's because, seven comes after sex.

I was terrible at playing baseball.
I couldn't break a window to save my life.

My closest friend moved to India.
Now, he's my farthest friend.

They asked Mike Tyson what he used when he went fishing.
He said a left hook.

I asked my wife if there was another man.
She said, "Of course not! He's not even 21 yet."

People still ask where I was when President Kennedy was shot.
Do I still need an alibi?

My friend complained about his half-brother,
So I said, "You can't half pick your relatives"

In a sushi restaurant, does the waiter say, "And how un-cooked would you like it?"

With the end of the space shuttle program, NASA announced plans to retire Major Tom.
Tom was informed this morning by Ground Control
(Ground Control to Major Tom)

Information about the Axe Murderer was stolen from the police department's computer.
Apparently the Axe Murderer's files were hacked.

I asked The Eagles why they wrote that song,
"I Can't Tell You Why".
They said that information was confidential

(They can't tell me why, no, no baby…)

How come armored cars look like trucks?

If one more person calls me "Shorty",
I'm going to punch him right in the shin.

The old gray mayor just ain't what he used to be.
I don't think that he'll get re-elected.

I can't believe how much they're charging for Parking nowadays.
It cost me two hundred and fifty dollars to park in that handicap spot.

The bike club members asked me if I ever did a century ride.
I said, "Yes, I rode into the 21st century."

It's not unusual for a singer to have his own theme song.
It's not unusual. Like Tom Jones. "It's not Unusual"

Talk about obesity in children, I knew a kid whose butt was so big, it took a half an hour to spank him.

Do you know what Cary Grant's favorite TV show was?
"Punch and Judy, Judy, Judy"

They asked me if I went out on my wife last night.
I said, "No, it was girl's night out."

To help with the war effort,
The president wants to send Kim Komando over there.

The economy is so bad in my household that it's even affecting my dog.
I'm having to Ration its Kennel.

In fact, things are so bad that I'm having to feed my dog Gravy without the Train.

I asked the guy how long he had been out of work.
He said that he hadn't had a job in two years.
I said, "And you didn't turn to robbery?"
He said that he hadn't pulled a job in two years.

I bought a car from a celebrity.
I've got Tiger's former Caddie.

One option they considered for the TV show was to kill off the entire cast and rename it, "Two and a Half Dead Men"

36

There's a new TV show about a group of people who cannot have sex in the traditional manner.
It's called, "Missionary Position Impossible"

Back when Hodgkin was still alive, a man said to him,
"Hodgkin! I have your disease."
Hodgkin said, "I feel your pain."

I've got one of those "Pay as you go" cell phones.
After the first bill, I realized that I've got to stop going.

In golf, you have to hit the ball from wherever it lands.
I should have brought a bathing suit with me!

When I bought my new electric car, the salesman said that it had "Power everything".
The next week, I called him up and said, "Why is the battery always dead?"
He said, "Because it has Power everything."

They asked Tiger Woods if he ever cheated on the golf course.
He said, no... he always got a hotel room.

My wife made a confession to me last night.
She said that she really doesn't play Bridge with her friends every Friday night.
Instead, she puts on a dark haired wig and goes out with my twin brother.
Remembering that I don't have a twin brother, I said, "So that's you?"

A guy threatened me by saying, "You're a dead man!"
I said, "That's up to the coroner"

They asked me how I knew that I was heterosexual.
I said that my wife told me.

I had to cut my vacation short because I wasn't tall enough.

The Psychic asked me if I believed that he could read minds.
I said, "You tell me."

They asked me why they always hear quacking in my bedroom.
I said that I owned a Dux bed.

In all the pictures of me, they asked why my lips always form an "O".
I said that I was on a low fat diet, so I always have to say, "LOW fat cheese"

My new female doctor asked me if I was able to have sex.
I said, "No. I'm married."

I'm really good at playing Bridge.
Everybody walks all over me.

The prison wants to bring in a rock group to entertain the death row inmates.
They've signed The Gas Chambers Brothers.

My bully co-worker said that he was going to knock me into next Wednesday.
I said, "Great! That's payday!"

I've never ridden in a limo.
I take a backseat to nobody!

That Rod Stewart sure is getting old.
Have you heard his latest song?
"Do ya think I'm sixty? Do ya think I'm sixty…"

They told me that I had a chip on my shoulder.
I said, "I know. I'm going in for surgery next Tuesday"

I noticed that I wasn't getting any phone calls, so I called the phone company.
They said that I was on a "Do not call" list.

I know a carpenter who is really depressed.
All of his door nails are dead.

The doctor explained the risky procedure by saying, "This operation may cost you your life."
I said, "Well, that's cheaper than I thought it was going to cost!"

I used to pay attention, until I found out how much they were charging for attention!

I confess that sometimes I wear my wife's clothing.
Luckily she dresses like a man.

I hate this law against texting and driving.
Now, I'm having to write everything out in longhand.

I can't shop on the Internet anymore.
PayPal, un-paled me

Dolly Parton is endorsing a new brand of shampoo.
It's called, "Head and Boulders"

Have you ever said that you're going to do something until the cows come home…
and the damned cows come home immediately?

With this economy, I'm even under water with my father.

I owe him more than he's worth.

My hot tub sprung a leak.
Now, I have a hot yard.

They asked me if I had a higher education.
I said, "Yes, I went to college back in the seventies"

I'm going to miss REM.
It was the only rock group that I could spell.

My cardiologist said that I couldn't eat ice cream anymore.
I asked, "Can I get a heart transplant?"
He said, "That's pretty extreme!"
I said, "That's what I'd do for a Klondike Bar!"

I shot my plasma TV, even though it wasn't doing anything wrong.
I shot it in cold plasma.

If I write my own obituary in the third person,
does that mean that all three of us have to die?

They asked me why I don't tell my jokes to Protesters.
I said that I don't want to cause a laugh riot.

They asked me how old Phillip was.
I said, "Phillip's 66"

My cat doesn't eat Tender Vittles anymore since I took down the bird bath.

Today I learned that if your leg falls asleep,
it doesn't help to say, "Cock-a-do-do-do!"

I told my doctor that I can't sleep all night.
He suggested that I stop sleeping all day.

I decided that if I'm ever lost in the desert, I'm going to give up drinking.

When I was back in school, the teacher asked the class,
"How many of you can't count?"
I raised my hand and said, "Six!"
"... Seven?"

I see that Tiger got a new sponsor. His only line in the commercial is,
"They're grrrreat!"

I notice that they erected a permanent sign on the freeway:

"Welcome to Marin County. Road under construction"

You know that sign saying, "Double fine for speeding in a construction zone"
The speed limit is fifty-five, so if I'm going to get a double fine, I might as well go a hundred and ten.

You know, I'm nice to those road construction workers when I drive by.
I always call out to them, "Hey, slow down!"

My wife said that I have no taste in clothing.
I disagreed and ate my shirt.
…It tasted like chicken.

My doctor's a real comic.
He's Rex Morgan.

The caller asked if I was willing to take a survey.
I said, "Is that the only question?"

If somebody is perfectly sane, why don't people describe him by saying,
"The lights are off and everybody's home"
Or
"The elevator stops on every floor"

This rotator cuff problem is keeping me from Protesting.
I can't throw a brick to save my life.

I see that Justin Bieber has been hit with a paternity suit.
Leave it to Bieber.

They asked me if I found a silver lining with the Great Recession.
I said yes, but I sold it.

I got this chart to study for my eye test.
Let's see, the M is pointing up, the M is pointing that way…

We used to refer to the homeless as bums or hobos.
Now, we call them our neighbors.

When the new "Charlie's Angels" was canceled, they told the girls in person,
However they told Charlie over the phone.

My boss said the he was sensitive to my concerns.
Laughter is a "sense", isn't it?

I did my comedy act for John Bohner and he loved it!
He cried through the whole thing.

40

When a boy is young, he refers to his mother as his "old lady".
When he gets married, he refers to his wife as his "old lady".
Poor Oedipus! He only had one "old lady".

I became suspicious of our local cannabis clinic when I noticed that their attending physician was
Doctor John.

My doctor is a gambler. I told him that I was too young to die.
He said, "Wanna bet?"

Can you park in a handicapped spot if your car is disabled?

My bank is charging a new fee.
Now, new customers have to pay twelve ninety-five for the toaster.

I lost every gear in my transmission except Reverse.
Now, I have nothing to look forward to.

My doctor told me that I may have to look at death, straight in the face.
I said, "Just a second. Let me get my glasses."

Our local fast food joint installed a new drive through window.
You should have seen their faces the first time I drove through it!

You know, I just realized how dumb it was to go out and get flesh-colored tattoos.

After being stitched up for a laceration,
My doctor told me to cut down on cuts.

I always thought that if I drove safely, nothing bad would happen to me.
Well, guess what? I hit one of those "Drive Safely" signs.

When we got married, my wife told me that she wasn't going to use my name.
I couldn't understand that. I mean, "Joe" is a very nice name.

I guess it would be a problem if somebody called up and asked to speak to Joe.
We'd have to say, "The man or the woman?"

Here is the first historical attempt at "Gallows Humor":
"Hey, Tom Dooley! Wanna hear this new song I made up?"

Boy, this "Occupy" movement is really growing.
I went into a public restroom and the door on every stall said, "Occupied"

If you use Viagra and you have an encounter with your contemporary,

41

what do you do for the rest of the three hours and fifty five minutes?

They asked me how I've been married for so long.
I said, "I don't know."
They said, "How could you possibly not know?"
I said, "That's the answer that I always give":
        'Where's the newspaper?" - "I don't know"
        "Who left the door open? - "I don't know"
        "Are you going to mow the lawn?" - "I don't know"

I work with a number of young people and I want to fit in,
so I started wearing my pants half way down…, you know, the same way they do.
You know what I found out? You're supposed to wear underwear when you do that!

My doctor told me to stop smelling coffee.
It's okay to wake up. Just don't smell the coffee.

I watched one of those woman's softball games.
Boy, those ladies can pitch!
I sure wish that I could throw like a girl!

When I lost my job I had to open an account with
"No Pay Pal"

A lady used to tell me, "A woman's work is never done."
Then, she got laid off.
Guess what? (a woman's work **is** done)

You know who was one of the biggest liars?
Ripley, believe it or not.

I found out something about becoming a proctologist.
With those gloves, one size fits all.

They asked me why it took me so long to shave.
I said because I was two faced.

They asked Alexander Graham Bell what his first phone number was.
He said, "One."
They asked him what the first phone number that he called was.
He said, "Two"

I have to question this whole medical marijuana thing.
I mean, why would I want to go see a doctor who's loaded?

My Father used to say, "I don't have an estranged son. I have a strange son."

They asked me if I wanted to take a poll.
I said, "How long is the poll?"
They said about six feet.

They asked me how much I spent on that speed reading class.
I said that I was still reading the invoice.

To solve the financial problem in the Vatican,
the Pope announced a special 'second collection' next Sunday.

I hoping to get a 'hole digging' machine for Christmas,
So I've asked Santa for a Back Ho Ho.

At five foot, six, I have to look up when talking to really tall people.
We have lengthy discussions.

I was confused when the teacher explained what Moses did, so she asked,
"What parting of the Red Sea don't you understand?"

My friend said, "You only bought that vacuum cleaner because it's named after you."
I said, "That's ridicules." Then I ordered a cup of Joe.

Sorry that I'm late today.
I had to stop by the Dollar Store and get a bucks worth.

I just realized, if that TV show gets renewed for next season,
We'll *all* have to upgrade to Hawaii **6.0.**

I was warming up my singing voice...
"Me Me Me Me!"
... when my wife said, "It's always about You, isn't it?"

The doctor told me that I'd be healthier if I got a lot more sleep.
I took that as a wake-up call.

They asked the crook why he robbed the convenience store.
He said, "Because it was convenient."

Before I spoke at my friend's wake, my wife said, "Don't say anything funny."
So I said, "Let me read from my joke book...."

I get so frustrated with these weathermen.
Last night, one was talking about La Nina and finally I yelled, "Speak English!"

I got one of those combination detectors.

It's a fire detector, and it detects CO too.

My car failed the smog test.
I should have driven it to college.

I went to my kindergarten reunion and I was so embarrassed.
I cried when my wife left me off.

The doctor said that if I ever get ED, there's a vacuum pump available.
Wouldn't you know it? It's a DYSON.

I'm so bad at sports,
I'm even picked last to play *fantasy* football.
Then, the guys say, "Oh, *we're* stuck fantasying with Dyson!"

More bad news about La Nina.
It turns out that she's gay.

Can you imagine the luck?
No sooner do they allow gays in the military, they end the wars!

I'll always remember the bar fight that I was in last Thanksgiving.
I got the stuffings beat out of me.

Things are so bad nowadays that I'm having to cut back on everything.
In fact, my favorite football team is now, the THIRTY-Niners.

I went to school in Florida, which is why my grades were only average.
I was at C-Level.

Boy, did I embarrass myself at the hospital yesterday.
Before the procedure, I thought they told me to give myself an enigma.

I guess I'm not a member of the 99 percent anymore.
I got a 1 percent raise.

Every 'thankless' job is also a 'your welcomeless' job.

I'm often asked why I don't used canned laughter on my comedy recordings.
I can't make the cans laugh.

I found out what one of the big rock stars eats for breakfast.
Hall and Oatmeal.

Then, there was singer Ike Turner.
He enjoyed WheatTina.

44

And me? I have my breakfast at noon time.
I eat Captain Lunch.

I insulted a young person yesterday.
I said, "How can you walk with your pants pulled down that far?"
He turned around and crawled away from me!

I broke my wife's favorite vase, and I didn't know how to tell her,
So when she came home from work, I said, "I have breaking news!"

Actually, I always try to be good,
because someday, I want to Occupy Heaven.

Great news from Iran today, as they've decided to abandon their plans to create the
Nuclear Family.

They asked me how long I've been a Chevy Man.
I said, "Since I was a Chevy Boy."

They asked me what I've seen in my Chevrolet.
I said, "The USA"

Boy, this "Occupy" movement is really growing.
I drove past a KOA yesterday and there were tents everywhere!

Last month I applied to replace the guy who did that last minute on "60 Minutes",
but they turned me down, opting to rename the program, "59 Minutes".

I need to advance my education, but I can't afford university tuition,
So I've enrolled in the Community College of Phoenix.

I'm on a low fat diet, so the doctor told me that if I keep eating pizza, it will kill me.
I said, "Before or after the heart burn?"

Actually, my health has its ups and downs.
Every night, I'm bedridden for up to eight hours!

Marlo Thomas actually started as a child actress.
Her first show was called, "That Little Girl"

Bonanza originally was going to have three sons and a daughter:
Adam, Hoss, Little Joe and Angela Cartwright.

Do you know what the Number One song is in Afghanistan?
"Allah Didn't Make Little Green Apples"
… and it don't rain in East Kabul in the summer time…

I can't believe this birth certificate stuff with Obama.
Now, they're saying that his parents were Barbie and Kenya.

I asked my mother why she always spanked me on my birthday.
She said that I was asking for it.

My uncle always asks prostitutes if they are legal to work in this country.
If they say, "No,", then he asks which country they ARE legal to work in.

I understand that lawyers will be allowed in the Olympics.
They will leap over legal hurtles.

They asked Chaz Bono if he'd ever been a broad.
He said, "Once."

There's a new show about a guy who uses Facebook.
It's called, "Everybody Friends Raymond"

Can you go to a locksmith if you lose the key to your canned ham?

I asked my friend why he took so many over-the-counter drugs.
He said, because his dealer got busted.

My optometrist suspected that I was suffering from double-vision when I addressed
him as "Doctor! Doctor!"

They're going to update an old Glen Campbell song about reuniting with an old girl
friend.
It's called, "By the time I get Back from Phoenix"

I asked my wife if I could have an open marriage.
She said the subject was closed.

My wife asked me why I forgot to buy the Etta James album that she requested.
Instead, I brought home a package of cheese.
She said, "I specifically told you, 'Don't forgetta Etta."

Terminology has sure changed in the 21st century.
Now, if you have an X-wife, she's an Xtreme wife.

When they finalize a contract,
how come they never make sure that all the lower-case j's are dotted?

There are all those Smart Cars, and then, all of the rest of the cars.
So to bring them all in line, they've created a new policy called, "No car left
behind"

46

They asked me to name one of the Beatles,
So I named him Fred.

There's one word that you don't want associated with your family tree:
Timber!

My boss said that he had forgotten more than I'd ever know.
Then, he asked me who I was.

Boy, was I in trouble yesterday.
First, my wife wanted to have a word with me.
Then, my cat wanted to have a meow with me.
I'm glad I don't own a dog!

With this new on-line dictionary, we've finally found out Webster's wife's first name:
Merriam.

Did you see that Wikileaks is displaying pictures of naked women?
They're revealing Victoria's Secrets.

It has been decided that it's okay to paddle all school children.
The new policy is called, "No behind left behind."

They almost named that old lawyer TV show, "Hamilton Burger",
However, who wants to watch a guy lose every week?

My co-worker stopped talking to me.
Now, I have an ex-office spouse.

I asked my friend if he had ever questioned his sexuality.
He said yes, but he never gets a straight answer.

The Fed announced that the Interest rate will remain around zero for the next two years.
Well, thanks for nothing!

I finally have a good neighbor. A State Farm agent moved in next door.

After telling several jokes about bras, the lady said that I had a brazier sense of humor.

I heard about a horse with erectile dysfunction.
Mr. E.D.

The Catholic Church has changed the mass to use the more traditional version of Pig Latin.

"The Ordla be ithyouway"
"And ithyouway your iritspay"

I looked at the lady through rose colored glasses,
and noticed that she had rose hips.

If you dislocate your shoulder, why don't they relocate it?

That popular singer is going to put out a new, acoustical album called,
"Seal – Unsealed"

Marin County has an ecological coroner.
If you ask for a body bag, he says, "Paper or plastic?"

I didn't say that I didn't like the tall person's attitude.
I said that I didn't like the tall person's altitude.

When the Pope cooks dinner, does he use *Blessed* Virgin Olive Oil?
Extra Blessed Virgin?

When Jesus was little, did he ever say to Mary, "Mommmm!"
"Mother!!"
"Oh, come on, Ma!"

When they accused my uncle of driving under the influence,
He said, "You call *that*, driving?"

The cop asked my uncle when he had his last drink.
He said that it was 5 o'clock somewhere.

My uncle said that he'd been framed,
At which point, the judge pointed out that they don't frame mug shots.

They asked me what program I watched on the Playboy Channel.
I said, "The Sex O'Clock News"

They asked the news man what he was going to do on his date tonight.
He said, "Details at 11".

Everybody has heard the term, "Son of a Gun",
But nobody ever asks why Mr. Gun only had one son.
It's because he believed in Gun Control.

If the Lone Ranger was on Facebook,
Would Tonto "Kemosabe" him?

When Hugh Hefner was married, he let his wife use her maiden name:

Miss November.

They asked me if I had any skeletons in the closet.
I said yes and they're gay.

When I bought my mattress, I noticed that they charged me for half the sales tax.
I said that I specifically came to their store because the sign said, "WE pay the sales tax".
The guy said, "What part of WE don't you understand?"

When I asked my mother if I would ever get any taller,
She said that I should lower my expectations.

They asked me why I'm so good at writing on a blackboard.
I chalked it up to experience.

The dentist asked me what was wrong with my tooth.
I said that it tastes great, less filling.

They asked me if I ever ran away from home.
I said, "Lots of times, but my wife always finds me."

The economy is so bad that they foreclosed my *house*cleaner.

You don't want to give a parrot a lie detector test.
It will spend the rest of the day saying, "Polly want a graph test. Polly want a graph test."

While taking my driving test, I pulled around another car.
The instructor said that I passed it.

Do you know why we can't read the writings on the wall of pyramids?
Because they're encrypted.

I'm sure glad that "Password" isn't on TV nowadays.
Can you imagine Allen Ludden saying: "The password is asterisk, asterisk, asterisk."

I told my boss that I needed a raise,
So he gave me a phone book to sit on.

You don't want to dry off a soaking wet parrot.
It will spend the rest of the day saying, "Polly unsaturated. Polly unsaturated."

I asked the guy at the Mattress Store what memory foam was.
He couldn't remember.

I have a modern doctor. He said, "Take two of these and tweet me in the morning"

If the price of oats goes up any more, I'll have to buy an economy horse.

I have a question:
Is it okay to covet your neighbor's EX wife?

Do you know which oil company has the worst safety record?
Accidental Petroleum.

Roy Rogers used to scratch his horse with his itchy Trigger finger.

Can you get out of jail early for good behavior if you were convicted of bad behavior?

My mom told me that there was only one commandment that I needed to obey:
"Thy shalt not"

The really bad student died while taking a test. Instead of failing, he passed.

You don't want to watch a movie starring that actress in front of a parrot.
It will spend the rest of the day saying,
"Polly Bergen. Polly Bergen."

I went to the tire store for their 10-point check up.
Wouldn't you know it? They found 10 points in my tires.

I told my boss that he doesn't take me seriously.
Cracked him up!

I asked my tax preparer if he was licensed.
He said, "Sure. I drove over here."

If you're really thirsty, don't drink a glass of baking soda."

They asked me if my marriage was still working.
I said, "Yes, *she* is."

I lost my shirt at the track last night.
What the hell I took it off for, I'll never know.

I had no choice but to get my cat fixed.
I found out that he had nine wives.

The doctor told me to gain some weight,
So I ate his bill.

I found an occupation that does not require a drug test.
A drug dealer.

I'll always remember that line from the movie where the Wicked Witch of the West says to Dorothy,
"Oz didn't give nothing to the Tin Man!"

The doctor asked me to rate my pain on a scale of one to ten.
I said, "Ten!"
He said, "That's impossible. For a ten, you'd have to be unconscious...
Mr Dyson... Mr Dyson?!"

When I was little, I remember my parents having an argument ending with my Mother yelling, "Go to Blazes!" and stomping down to her bedroom.
Then, my Father left the house.
Now, as a little kid, I just assumed that; he was going to Blazes.
Come to find out, Blaze lived three doors down!

My friend had appendicitis, so I tried to cheer her up by telling her that she had "a cute" appendicitis.

When a dog thinks to itself, in its head, does it hear, "Bark! Bark! Bark! Bark!"

I asked the girl if I could see her again.
She said, "Sure, let me take off that blindfold"

I have to control my temper.
When the doctor told me to lose some weight, I lost it!!!

They asked me what I thought of those e-Readers.
I said, "F-Reader."

On that TV show, Jeopardy, there are two ways to answer questions based the segment of the program.
Let's say that the category is Prostitutes.
You could say, "I'll take Prostitutes for a hundred,"
However, if it's Double Jeopardy, you would say, "I'll take two Prostitutes for a hundred."

They asked me if I did any business in the *stock* market.
I said, "No, I'm a vegetarian."

I am so sick of these stores that say you can return anything, No Questions Asked.
I walked into the store to return an item and the guy says, "May I help you?"
Right away, a question!

I've been sowing my oats recently. Now I have an oat sweater.

It's tough getting older. My Doctor told me to cut down on salty language.

They asked me if I ever wore a hoodie.
I said, "No, but my car has one."

More bad news from my doctor.
He told me to stop using salt, especially when it's raining.
Man, when it rains, it pours!

My hair dye is so subtle that nobody's noticed that I'm using Scott's Anti-Brown.

I learned something at the cookout.
Don't try to barbeque potato chips yourself.

Clint Eastwood hired a housekeeper. The first thing he told her was, "Go ahead. Make my bed."

They asked me if I knew how to control my bladder.
I said, "That Depends"

The last time I asked a girl for a date, she told me that it was March 29th

Well, the divorce was finalized today.
They laid off my office spouse.

I'm having trouble with my sewing machine.
My Singer has started to Rap.

Your eyes are the windows to your soul.
They asked me if I was crying.
I said, "No, I'm washing my windows"

I hear that Facebook is adding a Spell Checker.
Now, if you type, "LOA", it says, "Don't you mean LOL?"

Sometimes, what seems like a good idea, actually isn't....
Like opening a funeral home in Death Valley.

The teacher told me that my spelling was atrocious.
I said, "Atrocious. A C T T R O CHOS...E?"

The doctor said that I should diet and exercise.
I said that I would, but I wanted to lose some weight first.

Do you know what meal they make out of sick cows?
Beef Not Well ington.

Today, they revealed Dick Clark's last words.
He said, "5, 4, 3, 2, 1..."

After the head transplant,
the patient didn't have the brains he was born with.

The guy who ran into my car turned out to be registered in my city.
I had a sex offender bender.

I told my doctor that I had a twinge.
He said, "Oh, does he look like you?"

My wife said that she would never leave me.
Thank goodness! We only have one car!

After hearing that my book was named, "Never Entertain During Watermelon
Season", they asked me if I ever actually had a watermelon thrown at me while on
stage.
I said, "You'll have to read the book to find out."
They said, "That's okay. It wasn't that important anyway."

The guy at the smog station said that my car has to give up smoking.

You know what you don't want to hear during robotic surgery?
"Warning! Warning!"

My foreign car was idling rough so I put a Chevy engine in it.
Now, it has an American idol.

It's funny how fixing one thing can cause another problem.
I called the doctor and said, "Doc, it's still working after four hours!"
He said that I was now suffering from "EF".
Erectile Function.

They asked Dick Clark if he was amazed by anything that he saw in Heaven.
He said that he couldn't believe how much weight Chubby Checker has lost.

He almost didn't recognize Fats Domino!

They asked me if I was going to get butt lift surgery.
I said, "No, it'll be easier if I just pulled my pants up."

The company I work for offers employees a 401K.
Employees for Kellogg's are offered a 401 Special K.

You know, cops sure say the dumbest things!

A cop yelled, "Put your arms down and your hands up!"
I yelled, "How can I put my arms down AND my hands up and still hold my guns?"

When I was young, I spent a lot of time being drugged.
They drugged me to school. They drugged me to church. They drugged me to....

The waiter asked me how I wanted my filet.
I said, "Minioned"

I've noticed that: All fish are sushi until you cook them.

They asked me if I knew what fear was.
I said, "I'm afraid so."

Many people think that the' right to bear arms' and 'freedom of speech' are linked together, and I agree. Everybody has the right to yell, "Please don't shoot me!"

I hear that Fleetwood Mac is going to record an updated version of an old song. It goes like this:
"Tsunamis only happen after earthquakes,
Flooding is synonymous with Tsunamis…"

There was a mix up with my lab work at the doctor's office.
Apparently he ran a pregnancy test on me.
I laughed it off until I realized that I tested positive.
I'm due in August!

You can tell if a dog is happy when it wags its tail.
Then I met a dog who had no tail, and he wasn't happy about it!

The next time we have a candle light dinner,
I'm going to blow them out before I eat them.

I asked the farmer why the cow was limping.
He said that the cow had pulled a calf.

My friend smokes like a chimney.
He hates "Spare the Air" days

The butcher told me that today's special was turkey wings.
I said that turkeys don't fly.
He said, "Okay, today's special is turkey arms.

I didn't want to admit to the guys at work that I had to sleep on the couch last night,
So I told them that I slept out in the convertible.

I found out that if you grow your hair, it doesn't hurt.

54

No pain, Rogaine.

I told the doctor that I had low t.
So, he gave me an upper case T.

They asked Dan Quayle to spell the word, "Tsunamis"
He said, "T I T L E   W A V E"

I asked the farmer why the pig was limping.
He said that the pig had pulled a hammie.

The judge asked the cop how he knew that the defendant had eaten the marijuana.
He said the he noticed his pot belly.

A guy said to me, "What if I dropped a bomb on you, right out of an F1?"
I said, "F2"

After pulling me over, the cop asked how fast I was going.
I said, "Apparently, not fast enough."

Since WWII, we've heard a lot about Winston Churchill,
But we never hear about Winston's brother, Marlboro.

The doctor said that I'd die if I didn't have the surgery, and he said that the surgery
costs twenty thousand dollars.
Then, he said, "Your money or your life!"

I was injured while hitch hiking.
Now I have to undergo Tommy Thumb surgery.

The doctor said, "If you're having chest pain, why are you holding your foot?"
I said, "That's what I dropped the chest on."

They asked me if I had ever been in Greece.
I said, "No, I tried out, but they picked John Travolta."

My taste in music changes as I get older.
I'm now into hip replacement hop.

After looking at a Johnny Mathis album,
Why is "The Twelfth of Never" only three minutes long?

I believe in that saying, "Never go to bed angry."
Last night I apologized to my bed.

I tried to get into music school but I couldn't pass the entrance exam. I got caught
on a trick, multiple choice question that said:

Select the name of a famous saxophone player:
A: Kenny A
B: Kenny B
C: Kenny G
I said, "G!"
Apparently, it was 'C'.
I never heard of Kenny C!!!

I told my friend that I took myself to the movies last night.
He said that I was dating myself.

I didn't take my former girl friend's advice and ended up in the Emergency Room.
The door hit me on the way out.

I was sick but I didn't have much money so I said,
"Doc, what's the cheapest way that you can make me feel better?"
So, he hugged me.
… Didn't cost a cent.
… I was so happy that I hugged him back.
… Made him feel better, too!

I like to sing when I work.
A friend asked me to help her move.
I sang, "Put your bed on my shoulders…."

Do people in the circus dream about running away and getting a real job?

The doctor told me to eat one more piece of chocolate, and then, never eat chocolate again.
On my next visit, he asked me how that last piece of chocolate was.
I said that it was bittersweet.

I bought this great new product, guaranteed to stop you from snoring.
You put in the ear phones, push the Play button and go to sleep.
Then, every 5 minutes a voice says, "Hey, cut that out!"

Recently, I've been having bad luck after I eat my breakfast.
Finally, I realized that I had bought a box of Unlucky Charms.

Sadness in the food industry today as the inventor of the expiration date, expired.

I look up to basket ball players.

My doctor tried to shock me by saying that my PSA reading was 6.2!
I said, "Doc, I've had earthquakes larger than that!"

After eating my raisin bran, they asked me why I always eat a second bowl of cereal.
I said that the second bowl was Post Raisin Bran.

I asked the guy why he bought an automatic rifle.
He said that he couldn't drive a stick.

I found out today, there's a big difference between going to Penn State
and going to the State Pen.

Regarding that football player, RG3,
Apparently if you call his family home and ask to speak to RG, they say, "Pick a number."

The one thing I hate about those new style pants,
is trying to fasten the belt over my knees.

In other countries, like Haiti, do they have a Sunday morning news program called,
"Face the Haitian?"

I drove to the tire store and complained, "I've only had these tires for a year!"
The guy said, "Yes, but it was a Good Year!"

You know which super hero that Superman has always avoided?
Green Kryptonite Lantern.

I bought one of those new, musical GPS units that sings out the instructions.
It still has some glitches, though.
Yesterday it sang, "No, I don't know the way to San Jose"

My cat lost some weight.
This morning, I vacuumed up at least a half a pound of her.

I asked my doctor how I could avoid depression.
He said to spend more money and support local businesses.

The Pope reached out to the Gay community today when he said,
"Do not covet your neighbor's husband."

A friend of mine asked me how my book sales were going.
I said, "Couldn't be better! Returns are up one hundred percent!"

Actually, I got royalty check from my publisher.
You know, you've got to read the small print on those things...
Like down at the bottom where it says, "Not a real check."

My attorney said that he was going to plead insanity.

I said, "You're crazy?"

My doctor advised against eating those little boxes of Macaroni and Cheese.
He issued "Small Kraft Warnings"

The government is warning about a little guy who pretends to be a doctor.
They issued "Small Quack Warnings"

They asked me if I ever ate duck.
I said that my Quack advised against it.

I got one of those new, musical GPS units for my car.
It sings out advice. Yesterday, it sang,
"Do anything, turn, turn, turn,
You're going the wrong way, turn, turn, turn..."

Sad news at my house last night.
I left my gate open and all my termites ran away.

My dog injured itself while performing a trick.
She had a roll-over accident.

After pardoning the 2 turkeys in November, the President invited them to
Thanksgiving dinner.

This time change has really affected my TV viewing.
Last night, I had to watch Hawaii FOUR O.

Bad News for the Al Juzeera Nework. The Bin Laden Videos have been canceled.

When Elton John asked his infant son what lady he wanted as his Godmother, the
baby said, "Gaga"

Steroids made Barry Bonds so big that he obstructed justice.

They say that William Shatner just turned 80, but I found him on Priceline for 70.

Charlie Sheen is being cast in a new TV show called, "Two And A Half Grams"

I got arrested in my bathroom for taking a WikiLeak.

To help with the Gulf clean up, the Queen has agreed to send all of her horses and
all of her men.

To prevent further damage, BP has set up giant booms around their bank accounts.

During a recent concert tour of Arizona, Jay and the Americans were asked to prove their citizenship.

Historians doubt that remains of Noah's Ark were actually found on Mount Ararat in Turkey, despite finding the name, "SS Noah's Ark" painted on the hull with a registration sticker that was 4800 years overdue.

Despite their recent problems, Toyotas still get the best gas mileage of any Recalled car.

Toyota's reputation is so messed up that Geico won't even give them fifteen minutes.

After the earthquake in Chile, I ran into the kitchen and yelled, "Tsunami! Tsunami!"
My wife said, "Baloney!"

When you spin the clock forward, how come everything doesn't move around real fast for a few seconds?

They once asked Peter Graves what his first TV show was.
He responded with "Fury"!

The Pope insists that he did not cover up sexual abuse during the filming of "The Flying Nun"

I'm confused. Should I buy my car insurance from the white lady with the lipstick, the cartoon lady with the pink hair, or the lizard?

On the old TV show, "Batman", do you know who performed the theme song for Frank Gorshin's character?
Nelson Riddler.

They asked me why I keep insisting that my hair is still brown.
I said that it was a pigment of my imagination.

I can't believe all the things that they make out of turkey nowadays.
There's Turkey Sausage, Turkey Burgers...
Why, yesterday, for desert I had Peach Gobbler.

All the guys talk about that woman's body.
She has a figure of speech.

The guy insulted me by saying that I couldn't walk and talk at the same time.
I marched right over to him and said, "Whoops!"

I can't believe that 15 years later, Tupac's music is still popular.

It just goes to show, you can't kill rap music no matter how many times you shoot it.

I found out something about my deaf uncle.
He's not a good listener.

I took inventory of my life today and discovered that I only have one life to live.

I noticed something about my dog.
She has a voice activated tail.

To me, my hair is still dark; however some of my friends are starting to call me, "Whitie".
You know which one of my friends isn't calling me that?
Baldy!

Each time Elvis finished his night club act,
How come the audience didn't yell out,
"You're welcome very much!"

My Aunt suspected that my Uncle was bi-sexual, so she asked him, "Is there another woman…. or man?"

I asked the guy at the mobile phone store why I'm charged for every minute that I use a land line, but the cell phone plan has 700 free minutes.
He said because you spend 699 minutes yelling, "What? What?" "Hello?" "Can you hear me?"

I'm using a new, terrorist deodorant.
It's called TaliBan.

You won't believe this, but my dog taught me how to swim.
That dog paddle is pretty easy to learn.

I can't believe how much prices have gone up over the years.
They're remaking that movie, "Butterflies are Free",
But now it's called, "Butterflies are Fourteen-ninety-five"

I couldn't get a job at the marijuana clinic.
Apparently, I passed the drug test.

I wanted to show my doctor how tough I was, so when he told me to prepare for the injection, I said,
"Go ahead, give me your best shot!"

I get so emotional sometimes. My wife said to me, "What kind of tree is that?"
I cried, "A Weeping Willow".

60

My parents were always sending me mixed messages:
They'd say, "Be happy with what you've got,"
But then they'd say, "You're going to get yours!"

That old TV show was almost called, "Take it or Leave it…. To Beaver"

A friend of mine works for Head Start, but he didn't go to work this morning.
He couldn't get his head started.

I told my friend that I was writing the story of my life.
She said, "But you've been working on that for over 20 years now!"
I said, "That's the story of my life."

They asked my uncle how he dealt with masturbation.
He said that he'd come to grips with it.

As a comedian, I was the opposite of Elvis.
During my act, they'd announce, "The audience has left the building"

I asked the hip replacement doctor what they did with the old hips.
He said that they give them to people who aren't hip.

I've decided to stop working out.
It's the end of my Physical Year.

While the guy was robbing me, he said, "Is that a good watch?"
I said, "Take it from me!"

The doctor told me to cut down on Grease.
There goes my trip to Athens!

I suspected that the guy was a former taxi driver
when he told me that he had a Checkered past.

They asked me why I've never driven a taxi cab.
I said that the guy always makes me sit in the back.

They put a new mat in front of the door of my house.
That was a Welcome sight.

The prostitute said to my uncle, "You're not going to change your mind and start
respecting me in the morning, are you?"

I signed up for this on-line service that reports the local weather. I just got this
message: "You've got Hail"

Years ago, I used to buy Tareyton cigarettes because the filters contained activated charcoal.
Do you know how many cigarettes it took to cook a hamburger?

When we got married, I seriously considered taking my wife's name.
But then I thought about always having to explain why name is Leslie Ann.

Attempting to diversify, Chrysler is going into the sporting goods business.
They're going to sell Dodge Balls.

I'm concerned about rising sea levels.
If the ocean rises three feet in a hundred years, my grave site will be flooded.

They asked me how long it took me to ride a hundred miles on my bicycle.
I said, "A Century."

If they lay you off from the Fire Department,
Does your boss run in and yell, "Fired! Fired!" ?

A car drove across my garden yesterday.
It squished my squash.

I got one of those new musical micro chips put into my dog.
Now, if the humane society ever reads the chip, it will sing,
"...and Bingo was his name-o."

I was so disappointed. I spent three days at Disneyland and never saw Mickey Rooney.

Boy, Tiger's at it again. While he was playing golf yesterday, somebody asked him how many girl friends he had now, and he yelled, "Four!"

They asked me when I said my prayers.
I said, every time somebody pulls a gun on me and says, "Say your prayers"

It was revealed today that jockey Willy Shoemaker wore custom made boots.
They were created by that famous shoe designer, Willie Horserider.

The Bank of Italy announced that the Tower of Pisa will never fall down.
They put a lien against it.

When I was young, they asked me why I went to college instead of working at the zoo.
I said that I was trying to avoid the giraffe.

I got this important looking envelop in the mail that said, "Dated Material Enclosed".

I said, "How did they get a copy of my material?"

Disney announced that they're remaking a classic movie, but with a smaller cast.
It will be called, "One Dalmatian with a Hundred Spots"

I avoid clinical depression by staying out of the clinic.

My friend said that his wife went into labor this morning.
I said that it was nice to hear that she was working again.

My doctor said that I was an accident, waiting to happen.
I said, "Man, maybe I should buy some car insurance!"

They asked me if I've been a vegetarian for very long.
I said that I didn't just fall off the turnip truck.

I've noticed that when my wife is out of town,
our cats curse a lot more.

My wife belongs to one of those "Adopt an older animal" societies.
Yesterday, they called and asked her if she wanted an old goat.
She said, no, she already lived with one.

I didn't know if I needed one, but then again, I didn't want to regret my decision
later on, so finally, I said to myself, "Look, if you don't buy this gun, you're going
to shoot yourself."

I've always had to use products to help me eat.
When I was younger, I used Tums.
At this age, I use Gums.

I met a couple of celebrities this morning.
I got pulled over by Adam 12.

I'm using this new coffee-flavored deodorant.
It's called YuBAN.

The vet told me that my cat was on its last legs.
I said, "Wait a minute. How can all four legs go at once?"

My doctor put me on a restricted diet.
He told me to stop doing anything for a Klondike bar.

The doctor examined Achilles' leg and said,
"You've torn your own tendon."

I can't believe how much money Geico just saved me.

They cancelled my policy.

When the store detective accused me of shop lifting,
I said that I was only window shopping.
He said, "Yeah, I see that window in your pants"

The vet performed surgery on my pet chicken.
He removed his giblets.

They arrested a guy for selling drugs at McDonalds.
They got suspicious when he started selling Quarter Ounces.

Some things never change. On Facebook, I sent my publisher a Friend Request,
and he sent me a rejection slip.

They asked me if I knew that the two ladies living next door were nudists.
I said that I'd look into it.

So, I hiked up switch back after switch back to get to the top of the mountain.
Finally, I opened up my camera and the message said, "Batteries are exhausted"
I said, "The BATTERIES are exhausted? I hiked up the hill!"

They asked me when I got my last new car.
I said, "Back when my car was new."

I got a recall notice, telling me to return my car to the dealer as quickly as possible.
Fortunately, that was the same day that it got repossessed.

I was listening to Marvin Gaye sing "Sexual Healing" and I had to wonder,
What sexual injury did he suffer?
Did he pull something?

I told my Daddy that if he didn't stop drinking,
I was going to start driving a hot rod Lincoln!

Some jobs only last so long.
Like this morning, my boss told me, "So long."

I hear that the Pope got a new GPS unit.
It's specifically designed, not to lead him into temptation.

James Taylor and Carol King have reunited and released a new song called,
"You've got a Friend Request"

A lot of people don't know that Marvin Gaye was riding a horse when he wrote his famous song.
"Whoa! Mercy, mercy me.

Whoa! Things ain't what they used to be."
Whoa! Whoa, big fella! Radiation underground and in the sky ...."

The doctor told me to reduce my alcohol consumption,
so now I'm drinking Seagram's 6.

The theater critic asked me if I had ever seen "Half a Sixpence"
I said, "Not at those prices!"

They asked me why I wrote a book.
I said because I know how to type.

My car mechanic thinks he's a doctor.
He told me that I needed a new rear end.

Do you know whose show isn't on TV anymore?
Dead Sullivan.

My wife thinks that I still have this thing for my former college girl friend.
I said, "I'm not interested in her any more. God, she's got to be as old as you
are............ I mean...."

In the courtroom, the Prosecutor asked me, "Did you ever have success as a
comedian?"
I yelled, "I killed them, and I'm glad I killed them, and I'd kill them again! Do you
hear me? I'd kill them again!"

It's nice to know that my wife can trust me as far as she can throw me.
Why, last night she threw me over a hundred feet!

I went to my banker and asked for a car loan.
He said no, he needed it tonight.

Do you realize that if "The Mod Squad" was filmed today,
only one of them would know how to rap?

I thought that I saw Kool, of Kool and the Gang,
However the closer he got, I realized that he was not Kool.
... he was unKool....

If something costs nine-ninety nine and it goes up by eleven cents,
How come it doesn't cost ten-tenty ten?

I could tell that my Grandfather's eye sight was going
when he kept trying to change the channel by turning the steering wheel.

They finally figured out how Lance Armstrong passed all those drug tests.

He had the answers written on his hand.

I was never very good at chewing tobacco.
I was always getting the paper and filters stuck in my teeth.

The vet said that my dog had ticks.
I said, "That's impossible. He doesn't even know what time it is"

I told the repairman that my clock stopped working.
He said that I shouldn't be alarmed.

I told my friend that when I go on vacation, I board my dog.
He said, "What did you do? Tell him your jokes?"

The kid working at the McDonalds hates me.
He's my Arch enemy.

I went to the Subway restaurant yesterday and the guy asked me if I wanted a foot long.
I said, "You can do that?"

My uncle had a shot gun wedding.
He's been married to that gun for over 25 years now.

In court, the judge said that I couldn't get divorced.
He said that I was sentenced to wife.

My wife asked me what she should do with my ashes when I'm gone.
I said to vacuum them up with the Dyson.

Somebody pulled a knife on Tiger Woods!
Fortunately, he missed the cut.

I asked the doctor when I could go to work.
He said that I should be able to start on Monday.
I said, "That's great, Doc! What time should I be here?"

I'll always remember that episode of "The Honeymooners" where Ralph finally did go, BANG, ZOOM! and Alice said, "One small step for man, one giant leap…"

I got a knife pulled on me at dinner last night.
That's the last time I'm eating sword fish!

They asked me how long I've been married.
I said, "Since last century."

When that former quarterback was little,

Did they call him, Baby Boomer Eiason?

I was driving past an accident scene and I was trying to take a really good look, when I realized… I don't have a rubber neck!

The most disappointing day of my early childhood
was waking up and realizing that the Impossible Dream really didn't happen.

They asked me why I never became a pharmacist.
I said that I couldn't pass the drug test.

They said that the Voyager spacecraft has flown to farthest portion of The Fifth Dimension.
(I mean, that one guy was pretty big)

Great news from singer/songwriter Michael Murphy.
Wildfire came back!
Remember, he busted down his stall and in a blizzard he was lost?
Well, he came back!

They ask me why I take my cat with me on vacation.
I said because I stay at flea bag motels.

I just looked at my marriage license. It says that I have to wear corrective lenses.

There is no truth to the rumor that I'm writing a song called,
"Don't it make your brown hair gray?"

The Pope says that Smokey Robinson cannot become a Saint,
even though he performed with the Miracles.

When my publisher said that they wanted to make an electronic version of my book,
I was shocked!

I asked my insurance man why he bundled my policies.
He said it was the only way that the trash man would take them.

Will Geico cover your claim if you run over a lizard?

They asked me why I like to hike.
I said because everybody keeps telling me to take one.

They asked me why I like to fly a kite.
I said because everybody…. Oh, never mind.

Yesterday, I met someone who spoke to me in my native tongue.
He said, "Goo Goo! Gaa Gaa!"

Should you apologize profusely if you're bleeding profusely?

The woman found out that her husband was cheating on her,
when the paper boy walked up and yelled,
"Extra! Extra! Martial affair!"

Oh, I have a tip for NFL players on how to convince the coach to let you back into
the game after getting knocked out.
Write on your hand: The name of the city you're in, the day of the week, and the
name of the President.

My wife accidently used my tube of "Just For Men"
You should see her mustache now!

The professor complained that nobody reads anymore, but I disagreed with him.
I said that at least 2 or 3 people had read *my* book.

My wife accused me of misconduct.
I said, "I don't even know Miss Conduct!"

Scientists say that Mars appears to resemble the east coast of the United States,
Especially after they discovered a sign that said,
"See Rock City"

They asked my uncle why he was smoking marijuana.
He said that it must be four, twenty somewhere.

I always wanted to be a circus clown but my Father wouldn't let me.
He was always saying, "Wipe that smile off your face!"

They asked me why I don't dye my hair.
I said that I was sick of people saying, "Hey, young fellow!" "Excuse me, young
man."

I can't believe the nerve of our local newspaper.
I wrote a letter to the editor,
And they published the damn thing!

How come the meter maid never dusts or vacuums?

I was going to start an anti-bullying campaign,
but the big guy down the street threatened to kick my butt if I did.

Somebody asked me if I was the star of that movie, "The Mummy".
I said, "No, I always look like this after I shave."

68

My barber is also my mechanic.
Yesterday, he changed the oil in my hair.

I asked my uncle if he wanted to declare bankruptcy.
He said, "Well, I declare!"

I found out why it's illegal to laundry money.
It rips apart during the spin cycle.

I was a little leery of the guy who offered to give me a crash course on how to ride a motorcycle.

I feel sorry for the guy who was driving that cruise ship that capsized.
The only person who has stuck by the Captain is Tennille.

Oh, I learned something yesterday.
Don't draw on your face with a septic pencil.

In church, the preacher was saying that you have to be 'called to the priesthood'.
At that very moment, my cell phone rang.
The preacher stared at me and said, "Turn off that cell phone."
I guess I missed my calling.

Scientists in Iran have been watching all of the old Batman TV shows because the Batmobile was atomic powered. Now, it's predicted that Iran is just two years away from creating their own Batmobile.

How come, when you're having the time of your life,
nobody ever asks you what time it is?
"Why, it's the time of my life"

I asked the dentist how to make my teeth look whiter.
He said to darken my mustache.

A lot of people don't know that one of the last presidential candidates had a dog.
Mutt Romney.

The economy is so bad it's even affecting the Internet.
Yesterday, I lost my home page.

I've never had any luck with girls.
Every one that I ever bet on, lost.

If you're not on a first name basis with Cher,
what do you call her?

On Halloween, I didn't go to work.

Instead, I went to the beach.
The next day, my boss asked me where I was yesterday.
I said that I was here at work.
He said that he didn't see me here.
I said that it was Halloween and that I was dressed as a ghost.
He bought it!
It sure helps when your boss believes in ghosts!

On Facebook, Puff the Magic Dragon got a Friend Request from Little Jackie Paper.
Thank goodness! He'd been in that cave for over thirty years now!

They asked me if I ever tried Rock Climbing.
I said, "Of course! How do you think I got so good at
Rock Falling?"

My job review said that I was wishy washy,
But that I wasn't Ishy Squishy.

My weight lifting friend wanted me to be in the Olympics with him.
He does the clean lift a jerk.

They asked me if I ever saw The Color Purple.
I said, "Yes. The last time I fell off a ladder. It was purple for a week!"

They asked me if I ever yodeled.
I said, "Only when I use Yahoooooooooooo!"

They asked me if my cat was acting any differently after the brain transplant.
I said, "I don't know. He won't stop barking."

They accused the lady of committing a misdemeanor.
She said, "I don't even know Mr. Meanor!"

You know the problem with those 5 hour energy drinks?
After the fifth hour, I have to wake up and drink another bottle.

My doctor asked me if I had given up sex.
I said, "No, I'm still a Male."
(What else was I going to be? Unknown?)

To save money, I've started buying those new, TIVO dinners.
That way, if I get hungry later on, I can rewind it and eat it again.

Hey, I found this great new soup called, Gold Bullion
Boy, is it expensive!!!
And I didn't find any carrots in it, either!

Advice: Don't shake somebody's hand during an earthquake.

I went to the post office to mail a letter to Gettysburg,
But I forgot to put down the house number and street name on the envelop.
The mail man handed it back to me and said, "Would you like to address this?"
I said, "Sure…. Four score and seven years ago, our forefathers…."

Many people don't know that they almost cast Jack Benny as the father on Lassie,
 But during the tryouts, Jack kept saying, "Timmy fell in the *WELL! Well!* Timmy
fell in the *well!"*

I did some upgrading yesterday.
I upgraded to Windows 8 and I upgraded to Seagram's 7.

You know what I found out yesterday?
Using your Smart Phone while driving your Smart Car
… is dumb.

They asked me why I don't say anything.
I said that it went without saying.

They told me that I could surf on my I-Phone.
I can't even stand up on it, much less surf!

I hired a guy to fix my gate,
So he nailed it shut.

My tax preparer has a lot of experience.
He's been around the H and R Block.

The hardest part about being a stay-at-home Dad,
is saying, "You just wait until your Mother gets home!"

You know the best time to give blood?
Right after you've been in a bar fight and thrown through the plate glass window.

We were talking about different types of singers, like Gladys Knight and Doris Day.
Somebody asked me what the difference was between Gladys and Doris.
I said that it was night and day.

They asked me when I cancelled my subscription to The Post.
I said on Saturday Evening.

I got in trouble yesterday. My wife found out that I went to a *Strip* Mall.

I was so disappointed. I bought one of those Fat *Free* Cookies…
And they *charged me* for them!

The doctor asked me how many trips I made to the bathroom at night.
I said, "Zero."
He said, "At your age, you don't have to make any trips to the bathroom?"
I said, "Doc, at this age, I *sleep* in the bathroom!"

They asked the lady if General Petraeus was a good lover.
She said she'd give him four stars!

My friend was so disappointed. She bought one of those Child Car Seats for her kid, and his feet still don't reach the pedals.

My agent convinced me to buy life insurance for my cat, but I had to get 9 policies!

Actually, I tried to buy a life insurance policy for myself,
but I didn't have enough money.
I couldn't pass the Fiscal.

I don't know about that computerized weather imaging systems used by the TV stations.
Now, they can show you exactly what time the storm isn't going to hit.

I was talking to my Indian friend and my Mexican friend yesterday.
I asked my Indian friend why he named his son, Krishna?
He said that he got the idea from Jesus.

The bully said that he was going to delay beating me up.
Instead, he said that he'd beat me up in a few weeks.
I said that he was just kicking my can down the road.

I hear that Ashton Kutcher was praised for his portrayal of Steve Jobs.
Everybody said to him, "Good Jobs!"

If Alfred Hitchcock had been on Facebook,
would we see his profile?

If you got a job in Greece,
did you get a Greece job?

The computer repairman told me to uninstall Foxfire,
so I turned to my fox and said, "You're fired!"

I found out that the mattress store demands payment, up front on all death beds.

If the Garden of Eden had been a giant computer room,
God would have said, "You can use any PC you want, but don't use the Apple"

How come, when a young man has two days worth of beard, he looks like a movie star or a model,
but when I have two days worth of beard, I look like I'm homeless?

Apparently, a few years ago General Motors tried to sell Saturn to NASA,
no rings attached.

I sent a letter to the Queen, asking how long it would take me to become a Knight.
She said, "Days."

My Doctor asked me if I was still interested in girls.
I said, "Yes, but most of them are young enough to be my granddaughters."

Times are tough.
Even my watch stopped working.

I asked my wife if she'd iron my shirt but she said no.
I got negative press.

I got this strange feeling that a certain show was on,
so I turned on the TV and there was an episode of "Psych".

Back in the day, you would have to wait a week to see the next episode of your favorite TV show.
Now, with "Law and Order" you just have to wait a half an hour.

Barry Manalow had an album called, "Songs of the Sixties"
Now, he has an album called, "Songs I Sung When I Was Sixty"

I just realized that I don't have a daisical.
I lack a daisical. I'm Lackadaisical. I don't have one.

Every morning, I go out and greet my car.
I say, "Hi Brid!"

The teacher kept me after school for typing in all Upper Case characters.
It was capital punishment.

How come, at the Spelling Bee, they never ask you to spell,
JELL-O?

What is a joke?
If you laugh at it,
then it's a joke.

A cop pulled me over and said, "Are you driving with a suspended license?"
I said, "Yes, it's hanging here on my rearview mirror."

When my watch broke, I took it to the Vet.
Mickey had a broken hand.

I haven't been to the movies in years.
So, I don't watch any of those movie award shows because I won't know anybody anyway.
In fact, somebody asked me if I was going to watch the Oscars.
I said, "Oscar who?"

My doctor gave me a list of things that I had to quit doing.
I said, "Doc! Every one of these things is what I would do for a Klondike bar!"

My wife asked me, if I'm ever close to death, should she pull the plug on me?
I said, "Only if I'm in the Electric Chair"

My wife said, "Is there another woman?"
I said no.
She said, "Weren't you out drinking with her last night?"
I said, "Of course not! She doesn't drink."

The old man was on his death bed.
The doctor asked him if there was anybody that he wanted to see, one last time.
He said that he wanted to see a prostitute.
The doctor said, "Why, of all people would you want to see a prostitute?"
The old man said, "Hey, wouldn't you want to see your daughter one last time?"

I asked the doctor how my uncle was.
He said that my uncle was in grave condition.
I said, "Oh no! He wanted to be cremated!"

They asked me if I was a God fearing man.
I said that I was afraid of the Holy Ghost.

How did we all know Batman's secret identity?

My mother had x-ray vision.
She was always saying, "You don't have a brain in your head!"

You hear those commercials, "9 out of 10 doctors recommend this aspirin."
Well that means that one doctor.... doesn't recommend it.
And they've found out something about that one doctor.
He has one hell of a headache.

The doctor asked the lady why she didn't want to have her baby at night.

She said that she was a day laborer.

I found out the most amazing thing about that singer, Babyface.
He shaves!

There's a new James Bond movie where he loses his eyesight.
It's called, "For Your Ears Only"

Do you know what they found out about "The Little Rascals"?
They were *gang* members!

I found out how to keep time from flying.
Stop having fun!

Since electric cars have caught on,
I see that electricity has shot up to four dollars per gallon!
Watt???!!!

You know what the most useless item is that you can buy?
A kite with no strings attached.

The kid standing outside the store asked me if I'd buy him six cans of beer.
I said, "Sure, as long as you give me one."
He said, "I'll have to see some ID on that."

The cop said, "Have you been drinking?"
I said, "I don't drink"
He said, "Can I see some ID"
I said, "You sound just like my bartender"

I found out something about those new computers.
The 'Touch Screen' doesn't work at a porn site.

If somebody steals my identity,
do I get my prostate back?

I told my wife that I wanted to retire.
She walked out to my car, came back in and said, "Your tires look just fine"

Do you know which president had the strongest stomach muscles?
Abbs Lincoln

I think that my mother was hard of hearing.
Every time I'd give her an explanation, she'd say, "What!!!!!"

My uncle was an exercise fanatic.
When he died, we had a closed casket funeral because he liked to do sit ups.

Those DUI tests don't make any sense.
How come they don't ask you to *drive* in a straight line?

My tires are going bald.
I can tell by the receding tread line.

They told me to "Shape up or Ship out!"
so I took up boating.

I never read "To Kill A Mockingbird".
I'm a vegetarian.

You know who looks just like your Father?
Father Time.

My uncle's sex life reads like an open book.
A phone book.

The vet asked me why I thought that my cat had amnesia
I said because she keeps saying, "Bark! Bark! Bark!"

There was a gas leak and it killed everybody at the party except for one guy.
He was the life of the party.

When I was young, I never drank beer that came out of a spigot.
I did everything possible to avoid the draft.

My VISA card expired. Priceless!!

My mother always read me a bedtime story.
Every night she'd read me the Riot Act.

There's a web site where you can type in the name of a singer and see if he's alive
or not.
I typed in the name, "John Legend"
It said that he was a living Legend.

Should you go to a psychiatrist if your problem is that you won't get off the couch?

They asked me why my favorite team was the Giants.
I said because size matters.

When a person says something that alarms you,
why doesn't a bell ring?

In order to compete with The Dollar Store,

Penny's is changing their name to "A Hundred Penny's"

I took a lie detector test.
It said that I was under oath

I was thinking of buying myself a hand basket,
Just in case I don't go to Heaven.

You know who's being affected the most by global warming?
The Ice Cream Man!

If you asked Sherlock Holmes a fairly difficult question, he would say,
"Junior High School, my dear Watson"
"Upper university, my dear Watson"

I asked the stoner what his favorite time of day was.
He said, "Twelve o'clock High, man."

Every year, we celebrate the anniversary of our first fight.
At this point, I don't even remember what it was about...
but my wife does.

Since my friend lost all that weight,
I haven't seen much of him.

My poor uncle is having memory problems... like yesterday he
started telling me a joke and forgot the punch line.
It's so frustrating too, because ... now I'll never know why
those two giraffes came walking into the bar.

I told the bully that I wouldn't fight him.
He said, "What if I gave you a Klondike Bar?"
I said, "Put em up!"

I just can't talk to my uncle.
I said I could do the task, but it would take X amount of time.
He said, "Why?"
I said, "No, it would take X amount of time."
He said, "Why?"
I said, "Okay, it will take Y amount of time."
He said, "Why Y?"
I said, "Okay, it will take YY amount of time."
He said, "Why YY?"
I just can't talk to my uncle.

I'm getting so old that I'm starting to refer to my old lady as
my *young* lady.

The Minister asked me if I had been born again.
I said, "No, my Mother said that once was enough."

My favorite baseball team went into a tail spin.
They've vowed to never ride in *that* airplane again!

I found out something at church last Sunday.
When the choir finishes a song, you're not supposed to yell, "Freebird!"

They asked me to do a word association:
Gram – I said, "Cocaine"
Ounce – I said, "Pot"
Pound – I said, "I can't afford it"

They asked me why I had the package between my legs.
I said that my doctor told me to lift with my knees.

To get more exercise, the doctor told me to do sit-*ups* instead of sit-downs.

My uncle is always losing things.
Like yesterday, he said that he lost all respect for me.

To cut down on sodium, the doctor told me to stop taking things with a grain of salt.

How come I only drive the car of my dreams when I'm
sleeping?

You can tell a woman's age when you ask her if she's on the pill,
and she asks you which one.

My watch stopped working.
That *ticks* me off!

They asked me where I got the second garden hose from.
I said that I ran over the first one with the lawn mower.

When you buy a horse,
why don't they tell you how many car power it has?

A lot of people don't know that Adam and Eve invented the first slogan:
"An apple a day keeps God away".

They added a new toll lane to the freeway in the morning and it's really expensive.
The cop charged me $240 for driving in it!

They asked me why I don't drive my car to school anymore.

I said, "Because it dropped out."

They asked me why it took me twice as long to shave.
I said because I was two faced.

They asked me if I had ever heard the Beatles song, "She Loves You".
I said, "Yeah, yeah, yeah"

The doctor told me that I had insomnia.
I took that as a wake-up call.

She said that we should get together on a Social Networking site.
I said, "My Face or yours?"

They sent the first dog into outer space.
He's the Mars Rover.

The time change always confuses me.
Do I have a four o'clock shadow or a six o'clock shadow?

Being a little guy, I'm always right!
It takes a big man to admit that he's wrong.

The Judge was barbequing at the picnic and asked me how I wanted my steak.
I asked the Judge for leniency

I learned a lot about the ocean when I was in school.
On each report card, I got seven C's.

How come I only drive the car of my dreams when I'm
sleeping?

Did Fatty Arbuckle and Fats Waller ever run into each other?

My car and I went to a funeral yesterday.
Our battery died.

I asked the optometrist what my problem was.
He said that I had visions of grandeur.

I have an addiction, and I have to see a special doctor for it.
I'm seeing a "rock and roll doctor"...
because I'm addicted to love!

I offended the waiter at the restaurant last night.
He asked me if I wanted stuffed peppers.
I did, so I said, ""Hey! Stuff it!"

(He got offended)

There was a song once where they said, "The Revolution will not be televised."
I get over 200 channels... and the Revolution will not be televised?

They asked me why I always wear a crucifix.
I said because I was a cross dresser.

They asked me if I ever streaked.
I said, "Back before I could afford clothes"

Boy, did I embarrass myself at The Dollar Store yesterday.
I didn't realize that I'm supposed to give *them* the dollar!

My wife doesn't like the word, "Edgewise"
She won't let me get that word in.

I go to a restaurant that has lousy service.
They asked me why I keep going there.
I said because I'm a lousy tipper.

I was cited once for being mentally undressed.

During his sermon, the Pope admitted that he likes Madonna.

Why do you have to pay for financial advice?

The doctor told the woman that she had to *pay up front* for her breast enhancement.

I embarrassed myself at my own wedding.
I thought he was asking me questions:
When he said, "Richer or poorer"
I said, "Richer!"

I ate breakfast at an Internet Café.
I had eggs and hash tags.

During my last physical, the doctor thought that he hurt me.
He was using that *rubber glove* when he said,
"What kind of car do you own?"
I said, "Audi!"

The barber asked me if I wanted to talk about my hair.
I said that was a gray area.

80

I asked my wife if she wanted to go out tonight.
She said no, she's been quarantined.

When the doctor told me that I had Whooping Cough,
I said, "Whoop! Whoop! Whoop!"

You hear a lot about Flipping Houses nowadays.
Well, I have a 3-step process for Flipping Houses.
Step 1: Unattach it from the foundation.
Step 2: Push on the side of the house.
Step 3:....
        .... you weren't buying this, were you?

The doctor asked me to rate my pain on a scale of 1 to 10.
I said, "1, 2,3,4,5,6,7,8,9,10!!!!!!!!!!!!!"

They installed one of those *automated* toilets down at my local tavern.
It *automatically* flushes when you're finished throwing up.

I went to the dog pound and adopted a *Greyhound.*
I'm telling you, I don't care how athletic that mailman is,
he doesn't stand a chance!
... he always comes in second.

I think that my doctor watches too many soap operas.
Yesterday he told me that I had one life to live.

I will now read the Last Will and Testament of Ward Cleaver.
"Leave it to Beaver"

I'm so disappointed with my exterminator.
He told me that this new process would not harm my pets.
I guess he didn't realize that I had pet termites.

I found out that my dog is Jewish.
After he bit the mailman, the fellow asked me if my dog had Rabbis.

I hit a tree with my car yesterday.
It happened so fast that I didn't have enough time to yell, "Timber"

The physiatrist said that I had a fictional girl friend.
I said, "Oh yeah? Then why does she get pregnant in Chapter Two?"

I knew that our relationship was in trouble when I asked her what time it was,
and she said, "The Twelfth of Never"

I found out something.
If you write a letter to the Editor of the newspaper,
Don't use the term, "Great Caesar's Ghost"

The doctor told me that I had a split personality.
I said, "I'm sorry, Doc, but the other guy wants a second opinion."

We've all heard the saying, "Sticks and stones will break my bones but words will never harm me."
What if those words are, "Break his bones!" ?

My boss asked me if I could do an all-nighter.
I said, "No, I normally have to get up twice"

I said that my life was an open book.
Now, if I could just get somebody to buy the damned book!

My friend said that he had poison oak.
I wanted to tease him, but I didn't know a poison **joke**.

They asked me if it was hard to install that new style window.
I said it was a double pane.

I used to hunch over when I walked,
but now I stand corrected.

Sad news from The North Pole.
They've discovered that Santa Claus' wife has turned to prostitution.
She's become a Ho Ho Ho!

If a psychiatrist comes to the conclusion that you're crazy,
does he tell you the diagnosis by saying, "*You're crazy! Crazy! Craze, Craze, Craze! Crazy!*"

You might have chosen the wrong psychiatrist,
if his office elevator doesn't stop on all floors...
or if his office light is on but nobody's there.

If your problem is that you keep repeating yourself,
don't go into the office saying, "Doctor, Doctor?"

When I was young, my mother wanted me to play the harp.
She was always harping on me!

They asked me why I painted tiny tuxedos on each of my bullets.
I said that I was using a sophisticated weapon.

82

I see that another celebrity is selling his memorabilia
Singer, Don McLean is selling his Chevy.
He said it was only driven to the Levee.

A young man asked me if I ever had long hair.
I said, "Yes, back when I was in college, I looked like Jesus"
He asked me how I knew that.
I said that every time I came home for the holidays,
my mother would look at me and say, "Oh, Jesus!"

I saw that sign, "Only **you** can prevent forest fires"
Well, thank God they're not including **me** in this!
Only **YOU** can prevent forest fires.
I mean, **I** don't have time to go out and prevent forest fires!
That's a load off my mind, boy!

The physiatrist asked me if I ever heard voices telling me what
to do.
I said, "I'm not sure, Doc. Let me ask them."

My friend told me that he and his wife **made love** while **flying**
in a plane.
I said, "What the flying f....."

I thought that I had a Celebrity Sighting at the supermarket
yesterday.
I said to myself, "Is that *Maryanne Faithful*?"
Then I got a little closer and realized that she wasn't faithful.
... I mean, she was Unfaithful, no, what I mean to say is...

I had a weird childhood.
Every time my Mother would say, "How could you be so stupid?"
I'd try to explain...

I asked the doctor what was wrong with me.
He said, "I can't put my finger on it."
I said, "Oh, go ahead, Doc. It's okay"

Since my friend lost all that weight,
I haven't seen much of him.

You know who's being affected the most by global warming?
The Ice Cream Man!

I called my mechanic and said that my car wouldn't start.
He asked me if it would turn over.
I said, "Not till I get it started."

They asked me if I ever saw "The Karate Kid".
I said, "Yes, and he kicked the hell outta me!"

The doctor asked me if I was having sexual problems.
I said, "Yeah, I lost her phone number!"

They asked me if I missed one month more than the others.
I said, "Yes, Miss April."

My cat got a ticket yesterday.
They got her for Kitty Littering.

I have a new computerized toilet.
Last night, it did a back up.

I found out that my favorite baseball player got cut.
He needed almost 20 stitches!

My friend asked me if I collected coins.
I said, "No, I have direct deposit"

I was asked where I found the ad for the used car.
I said that was classified information.

I've discovered something.
If you go out to pick roses,
don't wear rose colored glasses.

I was asked to describe the state of Florida.
I said, "There ain't no mountain high enough, there ain't no valley low enough...."

Am I the only one who thought that a Midwife
was the one between the First one and the Third one?

When we're growing up, we're all taught to say "Please" and "Thank you"
Why, as a kid, even Elvis Presley was taught to say "Please" and "Thank you very much"

I found out something today.
I have the same birthday as Methuselah.

They're going to make a movie with no dialog.
It's called "Speechless in Seattle"

My cat has a favorite movie:
"One Flea Over the Cuckoo's Nest"

I'm addicted to my bank.
Every day I go through withdrawals.

They asked me if I saw the *sleeper* wave?
I said, "No, I slept right through it"

How come The Endless Summer, ended?

They asked me why I typed my own name into Google Maps.
I said that I was trying to find myself.

I bought this new Toilet-Radio combination,
But the only thing it picks up is The **Flush** Limbaugh Show.

This **little** guy ran past us wearing **only his socks**!
When the cops asked me to describe him, I said that he was short and **socky.**

I said that I went to a fire sale.
They asked how big the fire sale was.
I said, "Three alarms"

You know, I can't get life insurance.
They say that the risk is too high that I'm going to die on stage.

With the invention of computers, they've found out that:
Half the kids nowadays, don't know how to do cursive writing,
And the other half doesn't know how to scribble.

I asked my uncle why he bought the filing cabinet.
He said because he was filing for divorce.

When they laid me off, I had to give back all of the company uniforms.
Luckily I was wearing my own underwear that day!

I've said it before, and I'll say it again.
I've said it before, and I'll say it again.

They asked me when the shooting occurred.
I said, "Right after the gun went BANG!"

My masseuse told me that I was **strong and handsome**.
He was massaging my ego.

I knew that the job wouldn't last long when they issued me a name tag that said,
"Goodbye! My name was Joe"

To ease my chest pain, the doctor told me to stop thanking people from the *bottom of my heart*.

They asked me if I ever thought about *all* of my ex-girlfriends.
I said every time somebody says, "Hey, how's what's-her-name?"

The doctor told me that I should eat more sea food.
I said, "I can't. I'm a vegetarian."
He said, "Then you should eat more sea weed."

You know, my act goes over the **best** on Halloween!
Everybody's out there yelling, "Boo! Boo!"

They asked me what I thought of that biblical movie.
I said that I walked out on Exodus.
I departed from Exodus
I found a way out of Exodus.

At confession last week, the priest said that nobody had ever admitted to doing *that* before!
I said, "I know. I committed an Original Sin"

You know, after writing this entire book,
I've noticed that nobody *ever* steals any of my jokes!
Imagine that!

The doctor told me that I can't eat chocolate anymore.
I said, "Well you may as well give me the lethal injection drug then."
He said, "I can't. Its chocolate flavored."

The representative asked me if I was receiving financial aid.
I said, "Not since my parents died."

They asked me if I was *over* my former girlfriend.
I said, "Not anymore."

My Anger Management Counselor asked me if I ever yell at anybody.
I said, "WHAT!!!"

I have a tip for you.
Don't ask your dog if he wants to get a bite to eat.

My Grandmother was telling me the story of her life:
How she came to America as a little girl went to school and met a handsome young man...
And at that point of the story, she passed away.
It's so sad, too because, now I'll never know if she got married and had kids.

… that's the part I was waiting for!

As a bicyclist, they asked me if I was worried about distracted drivers coming up behind me.
I said, "Only when I'm wearing my muscle shirt!"

My friend said the he felt on top of the world!
Then I bummed him out when I told him that we were ALL on top of the world.

I went to a job interview yesterday and I couldn't believe how dumb the interviewer was!
He said to me, "Fill out the app."
I said, "Aaaa, buddy! Don't you mean, *download* the app?"
How dumb can you be?
... I'm glad I didn't get the job!

The doctor told me to lose the love handles.
I'm sure going to miss that woman.

They asked me what I thought of E-cigarettes.
I said, "F-cigarettes!"

I said that I was on a liquid diet.
They asked me how much I've lost so far.
I said, "Two gallons"

The toilet backed up at my house last night.
It happened so fast, I didn't have enough time to yell, "Tsunami! Tsunami!"
… that was a big back up!
… oh, you know something? I found out that cats can swim!
...oh, is he pissed.

My car turned over a hundred thousand miles today.
That was the longest cliff I've ever seen!
It's still turning over.

My doctor uses the power of suggestion.
I told him that I had an upset stomach.
He told me to stop my belly aching.

My Grandfather lives in the past.
I asked him what day it was.
He said, "Yesterday!"

You know there's trouble if your "Check Engine" light comes on, followed by the "Bring your Check book" light.

A lady told me that her husband read my book and died laughing.
I told her that I was really sorry to hear that, and was she dating again yet?

They asked me if my idea to open a Fish Market caught on.
I said, "No, I didn't catch anything."

I got bad news.
The girl of my dreams woke up.

I can't keep up with today's fashions.
Like, yesterday I went out with a nose ring in my ear.
… I can't tell them apart!
In fact, I didn't realize it until I tried to blow my ear.

Does a Nudist ever have a dream that he's gone to the Nudist Colony and suddenly realizes that he's totally dressed?

Hey! Great news for Michael MacDonald!
In Colorado and Washington, they've legalized the
Doobie Brothers!

At the job interview, they asked me if I used drugs.
I said, "Only when I run out of liquor."

You know which former president might have been gay?
And, we should have known this, too.
The guy on the two dollar bill!

They asked me how my plan to open a Fast Food restaurant worked out.
I said that I wasn't fast enough.

They asked me the last time that I experienced Road Rage.
I said when my car wouldn't start and I said, "You pile of junk! You worthless piece of..."

It's tough now that my name has gotten famous.
Now, everybody thinks that I can fix their vacuums!

I worried about my surgery when I noticed that the doctor was eating a
Butterfingers.

They asked me if I ever had luck with the opposite sex.
I said, "Yes, I always have the opposite of sex."

I work for a non-profit.
My company hasn't made any money for years.

My uncle is using a walker nowadays...
Johnny Walker.

If a cop asks you when you started drinking,
don't tell him: back when you were sober.

The arborist said that my tree was on its last limbs.

If the post office is closed on Sunday,
how are they supposed to deliver us from evil?

I used the shampoo they gave me at the hotel last night.
How was I supposed to know that it was the "Yes, More Tears" formula?
... I haven't cried that hard since I paid the hotel bill!

They asked me how I got the flat tire.
I said that there was a fork in the road.

Do you know when a girl should get a headache?
Not tonight!

The doctor said, "Your medical treatment will include an operation."
I said, "What will you have to operate on?"
He said, "Your wallet."
... I haven't cried that hard since I paid the bill!

I finally found a psychiatrist who understands me.
He hates my mother too.

I've noticed something about Geico Insurance on the radio:
"You'll hear 15 commercials in just 15 minutes"

I took 365 vitamins this morning
I'm using this new brand called, "Once a Year"

During a routine traffic stop, the Police Dog started barking.
The cop proceeded to search my car, and sure enough,
he found my stash of dog biscuits.

You know the problem with Driverless Cars?
Getting them to come back.

My wife asked me if this dress makes her look fat.
I said, "No, it makes Me look skinny"

Now that he's no longer representing The Men's Warehouse,
George Zimmer has gotten a job at the Nudist Colony.

"You're going to like the way you look"

The doctor asked me if I was incontinent.
I said, "Yes, North America.
... That's the continent that I'm in."

I don't get mad often, but when the mechanic told me that my car had water in the oil,
I blew a head gasket!

When I was a kid, I played so many Beatle records
that we had to get the house fumigated.

My mechanic thinks he's a doctor.
He told my car to give up smoking.

You know, a lot of people say that *Tarzan* was a generous guy.
Why, he'd give you the loin cloth off his....

You can't trust people nowadays.
A guy gave me a quarter so naturally; I bit it to see if it was real.
Wouldn't you know, it was chocolate.

I hate it when people call me names.
Like yesterday, do you know *who* called me "Skinny"?
Fatso!

I can't go to Strip Joints anymore.
My doctor told me to cut down on Pasties.
.... Wait a minute.... He said, Pastries!

I bought one of those r*eusable* bags.
I took it the store and filled it with a bunch of food.
I brought it home and ate all the food.
The next morning, I opened my *reusable* bag... and it was empty!!
Reusable, my ass! Who are they trying to kid?

If you forgive those who trespass against you,
Are you still allowed to shoot them?
"Get off my land!" Bang! Bang! "But I forgive you"

I asked the doctor how to get rid of wrinkles.
He told me to wash with Woolite.

It's tough now that my name has gotten famous.
Now, everybody thinks I can fix their vacuum cleaner!

I worried about my surgery when I noticed that the doctor was eating a Butterfingers.

It's tough being an older driver.
The cop said that I was going the wrong way.
I said, "You mean I've had the wrong signal on all this time?"

There's a new show about two roommates who hate each other.
It's called, "How I Called You a Mother".

I hate it when women ask me hard questions like,
"What part of no don't I understand?"
How do I know?

I was thinking of dyeing my hair blond.
Then I thought, "Gee, that's a dumb idea!"

I see that my biggest critic is in the hospital.
He's on the critical list.

The cop said that one of my backup lights was burned out.
I said, "How do you know that?"
He said, "I saw it when you were backing into me."

The doctor asked me if I exercised.
I said that I exercise in futility.

The guy asked me how to get to the backpacking camp.
I told him to take a hike.

The judge restricted my license so I can only drive to work and back.
What a rip!
Now, I have to get a job!

After my last physical, my doctor said to me:
"You've got to stop drinking....
You've got to stop smoking....
and, you've got to stop cussing!"
I said, "What the..... what the.... "

My mother never believed me.
Even if I told her the truth she'd say,
"I don't believe it! I don't believe it!"

Hey, I found out how to get into Sam's Club.
Tell them that you're, Sam

....

My poor college football team had a horrible season.
First, they were defeated by Army.
Then, they were pummeled by Navy.
They were bombed by Air Force,
and they were massacred by The Seminoles.

... it's not like didn't have any talent.
They just didn't have any ...weapons.
You can't go against Army, Navy, Air Force and The Seminoles without weapons!

You just wait until next year!
....

I made up a password that was so complicated,
I had to call up a hacker to find out what it was.

I knew that I should be a comedian from an early age.
No matter what I said, my mother would say,
"You've got to be kidding me!"

When the judge asked me if I could prove that I was sleeping on the night of the crime,
I said, "Yes, ask Santa Claus"
.... because he knows when I've been sleeping, he knows when I'm awake...

I made up a password using the name of the girl that I met at the bar last night.
Now, if I could just remember what it was.

I have a co-worker who drives me nuts!
He whistles while he works.
Finally, one day I yelled, "Stop working!"

I've been using the same shampoo for years,
and only yesterday did I find out that,
you don't actually have to shampoo your shoulders.
... I thought those were directions.

I've discovered something about Motel 6.
You can't get the damned light to go off!
They'll leave it on for you, but good luck turning it off!
All night, it flashes: "Motel 6! Motel 6! Motel 6!"

I got a call from the dentist reminding me to get my teeth cleaned.
So I marched right into the bathroom and brushed my teeth!
...How did he know? The guy's a physic!

92

My wife asked me to be more open with her,
so I've decided to stay open until 5 from now on.
... and until Noon time on Saturdays.

If talk is cheap,
does that mean that Actions are more expensive than words?

My wife finally cleaned the house.
When she left, she took everything!

You know that your heart is in bad shape if your cardiologist suggests that you see the Wizard.

A lot of people don't know that I have a college degree.
I have a Bachelor of Fine Dyson....
or BFD.

I asked my Mother why she decided to have me.
She said that I was an accident waiting to happen.

You know, they had a lot of trouble with Lassie before she was trained properly.
In fact, her first movie was called, "Lassie, Come Back!" or "Lassie, Get Back Here!"

If you asked Henry Ford a difficult question, he would always defer to his son.
Like, they asked Henry Ford if all of his cars would be successful.
He said, "You'll have to ask Edsel."

When I was little, my Mother would encourage me to think.
She was always saying, "What do you think you're doing?"

My mother said that I was funny, even as an infant.
I would say things like, "These two babies come crawling into a bar, see..."

My dentist is always yelling at me.
It doesn't matter how much I brush or floss, the dentist yells at me.
Like, the last time I was there, he yelled, "When are you going to pay the bill?"

This year, I started to make a bucket list and I realized,
I don't need more than one bucket!

Phone numbers are so complicated nowadays.
Even for local calls, you have to dial one, then the area code and then the number.
Back in my day, you just had to dial M for murder, and that was it
.... today, it's, "If you know the murderer's extension, dial it now..."
... "If not, stay on the line for the next available murderer."

93

When my blind date met me, she said that she could only stay so long.
I asked how long that would be.
She said, "So long."

I found out something today.
Huckleberry Finn's dog was not named Huckleberry Hound.

I've never had to buy an ultimatum
People are always giving them to me.

If gas prices get any lower, you'll be able to buy it at The Dollar Store.

I met some women at the Nudist Colony who were so ugly,
I was mentally dressing them.

The cop asked me, "Isn't that an under aged lady?"
I said, "No, she's under the influence of age."

They asked me what day comes after April 30th.
I said, "Mayday! Mayday!"

My mother was always concerned about my mental health.
She was always saying, "Are you crazy?"

They asked me to give an example of "Supply and Demand".
I said, "Get those supplies in here, right now!"

I *promise* that I will never make any more *empty promises*.

They asked me if I ever saw "The Color Purple"
I said, "The last time I drank grape juice"

The interviewer asked me if I had ever *taken* drugs before.
I said, "No, I always paid for them."
…I've never *taken* drugs.

My Mother was always giving me math problems.
She'd say, "If I've told you once, I've told you…"
And I'd say, "A hundred times? A thousand times? A million times?"

They asked me why I played the radio so loud in my car.
I said, "What?"

Instead of being cremated, I told the funeral director that my uncle wanted to be buried.
He said, "I can dig it!"

94

The funeral director asked my uncle if he wanted to discuss his own funeral arrangements.
He said, "I don't think that's issue right now, however, how much would a funeral cost, anyway?"
The funeral director told him and he dropped dead.

They asked me why I only chopped down trees in freezing weather.
I said because I like to shiver me timbers.
Timmmmmmmberrrrrr!

My Mother liked to show me how tall she was.
She was always saying, "I've had it up to here with you!"

If you're changing a flat tire and a cop drives up,
Don't say, "This is a car jack"

The guy told me that he had an *artificial* hip.
I said, "Unreal!"

We had a fire drill at work yesterday.
They fired everybody!

They asked me if I had a criminal *record.*
I said, "No but some of my videos have been." (criminal)

I'm starting to get recognized around town nowadays.
People are always saying, "Oh, it's *you* again!"

Can you imagine if Superman *and Clark Kent* got married.....
to *different* women?
That would be Super!

I just found out,
Don't hitchhike in the Carpal Tunnel.

They asked me how many times I failed the math test.
I said that I had lost count.

I asked my young friend, "If you drop out of high school, where will you get your education?"
He said, "Just a minute, let me Google that."

I asked my neighbor to stop using that *Leaf Blower.*
He blew me off.

It was reported that when they *found* the *convict,*

hc said, "Well, I'll be *con*founded!"

My boss said that he was eliminating my position.
I said, "You mean, I can't sit down anymore?"

They asked me where the tools were.
I said I was clueless.
They asked me where the screws were.
I said I was screwless.

I think these Geico commercials are sending the wrong message.
A guy hit me yesterday so I asked him if he had insurance.
He said, "No, but give me 15 minutes, will ya?"

They're not going to build the Detox Center.
They were talked out of it.

To encourage me to save for retirement, my Mother would tell me the story of the squirrels. How all of the squirrels would spend the summer finding nuts and storing them for the winter, but one squirrel just ran around and played.... and when the winter came all of the squirrels went into their dens with all of their nuts, but that one squirrels had no nuts saved and he froze.
Well, here I am nearing retirement, and I don't have a penny saved....
but I do have sixty thousand pounds of nuts!

During the Job Interview, I asked the man if they offered benefits.
He said that they'd give me the benefit of the doubt.

My wife has several pet names for me:
Rover, Fido, Spot, Big Fella....

All of the tellers at the bank took their clothes off.
That raised my interest rate.

I am not in favor of medical testing on animals.
Then, my doctor said that I was going to be the first one to ever receive this type of surgery.
I said, "Hey, Doc, maybe we should try this on Fido first"

The tax judge said that he was going to garnish my salary.
I said, "Your Honor, I don't even garnish my salad!"

I was thinking of writing a song called, "By The Time I Get To The University Of Phoenix."

The Acme Muffler Factory burned to the ground today.
Muffler officials are baffled.

96

Fireman said that it was one of the quietest fires that they've ever fought.

Tonight on FOX, House buys a car so he has something to park in front of himself.

The military introduced a new weapon, which they intend to fire at the enemy.
It's called the Dodge Dart.
Said officials, "We can take out several of them at once if they stand in a straight line."

The Beatles were inducted into the Insect Hall Of Fame today,
joining other members, Hal Roach and Aunt Bea.

Legendary painter, Sherwin Williams gave up his lifelong plan to cover the earth today.
Said a pale blue Williams, "With all that ice melting, I can't get anything to stick."

The Tetley Tea Company reported a serious breach in security
today as several large tea leaves were smuggled into the facility.
Said Tetley officials, "Apparently, they cut them up in an effort to make them
appear as if they were tiny little tea leaves."
The company assures the public that none of the large tea leaves made their way
into the production line.

Tonight on FOX, after learning that he's going bald,
House gets a new roof.

Legendary singer, Bobby Goldsboro was arrested today for the
murder of his wife, Honey over forty-five years ago.
As officers put him in cell, he kept yelling,
"The angels took her away! The angels took her away!"

With the latest shortage of corn, we've all been asked to *care* if Jimmy cracks corn.

Singer Bobbi Gentry was arrested today for the murder of Billy Jo McAllister.
She is accused of pushing him off the Tallahatchie Bridge back in 1969.
For years, the death was listed as accidental until police determined that she just
knew too darned much about the case.
Gentry has appealed the ruling while asking the judge to pass the biscuits, please.

U.S. officials have announced that the border fence is almost complete.
In a related story, Mexican officials announced a growing national interest in the
sport of pole vaulting.

The original copy of the video game, "Grand Theft Auto" is missing.
The developer had left the copy in his car, which was stolen overnight.
The developer is currently working on a new game called,
"When I Catch The Son Of A Bitch".

Freddy Mac's house was foreclosed today.
He said, "I probably shouldn't have gotten an adjustable mortgage."
His wife, Fanny Mae is devastated as they search for a new place to live.
The couple is raising Fanny's two children,
Behind and Buttocks.

With the steroid problem solved in baseball, now a new drug is showing up.
Investigators said, "We noticed an increase in the size of the player's rear ends.
Now, we've discovered that many players are taking Asteroids."
The hope is to stop this trend before it spreads to football and their centers.

Two second fiddles have decided to unite and form a new singing duel named,
"Peaches and Messina".

To save the international athletes travel expenses, next years
Boston Marathon is going to be held in Kenya.

Years ago, Elton John rewrote one of his songs in honor of Princess Di.
Now, he's been asked to convert one of his songs in honor of the victims of 9/11.
The new song will called, "Bin Laden And The Jets"

Children's Hospital was shut down by the state today for operating with under age
doctors. Patients were transferred to nearby Adult Hospital.
Officials asked, "How can surgery be performed by doctors who don't even shave?"

DNA tests have revealed that Tom Dooley was not guilty after all.
Dooley, who hung down his head over fifty years ago, always claimed that he was
nowhere near that mountain and that he didn't own a knife.
For compensation, Dooley's relatives are being given a white oak tree.

Singer, Neil Diamond was pulled over for driving in the commute lane today.
He complained to officers, "But the sign says it's the
Diamond Lane!"

Back in prehistoric times,
These two dinosaurs come walking into a cave, see?
One dinosaur says to the other dinosaur,
"What if… one day all the dinosaurs died and over the years, their bodies became
oil and then, people built cars and ran them on gasoline that they'd made out of
oil… "
The other dinosaur interrupted,
"People?"
He responded, "Hey! I said, What if?"

At one time, they asked the world's oldest "fifties teenager", Dick Clark,
"What do you think of the high price of wheat?"

"Well, it cost more bread than it used to."

Well, I spent my day, Water Boarding. It's not that bad.
Of course, I had to tell them everything I knew before they'd stop...
but that didn't take too long.
As I was leaving, they gave me an autographed picture of Lloyd Bridges, Water Boarding.

Legendary actor Jay North was arrested today for a variety of offenses dating back to his childhood.
Former neighbor Mr. Wilson was usually the target of North's antics with most occurring between 7:30 and 8 PM on Sunday nights.
After Wilson's death, North's crime spree continued and has been chronicled in daily newspapers ever since.
Known as Jay the Menace, he confessed, "I was young. I needed the money."

The sons of the late legendary singer Ricky Nelson have opened a trucking company. Commenting on their new occupation, the sons replied,
"Dad always told us that he'd rather drive a truck."

Scientists have discovered large amounts of Rogaine in the nation's streams and ponds.
At the same time, park officials announced a significant change in the bald eagle population.
"I'd call it peach fuzz," commented one scientist. "But it's a start."

Historians discovered an unreleased song from the sixties by Gordon Lightfoot.
It's an autobiographical tune called,
"It ain't heavy, it's my foot".

It was reported today that Tony The Tiger, Snagglepuss, and The Exxon Tiger were all played by the same cat.
Mr. Cat was disturbed about the report being released and gave three comments to reporters. First he said,
"Well, that's just grrrrrrreat!"
Then, he said,
"Heavens to Murgatroid",
He finished by saying,
"That'll be eighty-seven, fifty please. Would you like a car wash with that?"

Today it was announced that singer Tony Orlando has moved and changed his name.
He is now known as Tony Tampa.
When asked if he'd done this before, the singer's wife, Dawn said, "Oh yes. Back when we lived in Oklahoma City."

They found out something about Ripley's Believe it or Not.
Ripley's Mother never believed it!

Do you know which baseball pitcher did this before every pitch?
(sigh)
Cy Young.

If singer, Simply Red passed away, how would they announce it on the news?
"Simply Red is simply dead."

In a recent barbequing accident, The Amazing Kreskin accidently set himself on fire.
From now on, he will be known as The Ablazing Kreskin.

The late Willie Shoemaker was honored at the racetrack today.
Shoemaker, who originally was a cobbler, was attracted to racing by the smell of shoe leather.
In a symbolic move, a rider-less horse ran in the seventh race and came in first, prompting officials to say, "Willie's still got it!"

Gangster, Killer Smith was laid to rest today. In a symbolic gesture, his body was pushed out of a speeding car as it passed the gravesite.

My doctor said that I needed triple bi-pass surgery.
I said that I'd like a third opinion on that.

Legendary singer, Seal donated his lips to a young fan who had lost his in an accident.
After the surgery, the young fan said, "My lips are Seals"

Tonight on Fox, *House* catches fire and finally gets a clean shave.

The housing crisis hit home today as The White House was repossessed.
Officials from the mortgage company, The Republic of China,
were changing the locks and telling their citizens that it wasn't really happening.
Speculation is that the structure will be converted into a China shop.

In the nation's capital today, the Lincoln Memorial stood up.
Said amazed tourists, "I never realized that he was that tall!"
The Washington Wizards immediately signed him to a ten-day contract.

The Tidy bowl Man was killed in a boating accident today in Flushing, New York.
"I'm surprised that he survived as long as he did," commented his close friend, Mr. Clean.
"He just couldn't stay out of the water."

In a related story, Mr. Clean revealed that he's considering getting hair implants.

Said Mr. Clean, "I'm getting sick of looking like a kid."
Then, he returned to cleaning the bathroom.

Further indication that our nation's military is stretched too thin when former
Marine **Gomer Pyle** was called back into active duty.
As officers dragged **Mr. Nabors** from his Hollywood mansion, he kept yelling, "It
was only a character that I played on TV!"

A guy came up behind me and asked, "Did you write "*Never Entertain During
Watermelon Season*" and, "*You and I are Intertwined*?"
I said, "Why, err... yes I did!"
He said, "Well, here's your books. You dropped them in the street back there"

I got kicked out of my favorite breakfast place this morning.
I ordered a bowl of cereal.
The waiter said, "Cheerio"
I said, "Ok, we'll see ya"

I went into the lumber yard and asked the salesman if he had treated wood.
He pointed over there and noticed a guy saying, "You stupid wood! You stupid
wood!"
The salesman yelled out, "Hey! Stop mistreating that wood!"

British officials admitted today that their famous clock is named after a man who
was married to two women at the same time.
They quickly renamed the clock, "Bigamy Ben"

I have a tip.
If you're homeless, don't tell the insurance man that you crash in your car.

If you don't smoke pot,
are you 420, unfriendly?

Was Gig Young's first name really Gigabyte?

In an attempt to keep up with its twin city, Minneapolis has applied for sainthood.

I went to a classic car show, and none of the cars were older than mine.

When asked what he thought of Sarah Palin, Bill Clinton said, "With or without her
glasses?"

The Fed is considering pressing charges against the wife of Barry Bonds' trainer.
They became suspicious after she hit seventy homeruns for the girls softball league
this year.

They told me to count my blessings

(Sneeze twice)
Let's see. That will be two.

I'm wearing one of those patches that help you give a damn.
It works. Now, all I think about is that damn patch.

Tiger Woods announced that he might attend The Ryder Cup while saying,
"I've got to rent a truck that weekend, anyway."

They threatened to put me in a Funny Farm.
Then, they saw my act.

A guy asked me if I wore a rug.
I said, "If I did, why would I choose a gray one?"

I always wondered what the cops would do if I ran away from them.
I was stunned!!

They rejected my application because I forgot to fill in the Street, city and state.
The guy said, "Location, location, location!"

As I've gotten older, do you know what I've discovered?
You CAN keep a good man down!

The doctor said that I had 48 hours to live.
I said, "Doc, doesn't the time change this weekend?"
He said, "Oh, that's right, you have 47 hours to live."

As I get older, I'm finding that my memory just isn't what it ... what it....

I'm sorry to report that Sleepy the Clown passed away.
They're not sure when Sleepy died.
It could have been this morning, but then, it could have been last week.
You could never tell with Sleepy.

Back when I was a kid, parents would call it, "Talking back"
Today, they call it a conversation.

Simon and Garfunkel have been asked to write a tribute song in honor of a famous
blues singer.
It will be called, "A Bridge over Muddy Waters"

How do you tell twins apart?
I can never tell if I'm in Minneapolis or St Paul.

My uncle went to get his Viagra prescription refilled.
The pharmacist said, "How much do you want?"

He said, "Eight inches!"

They asked me if sex was the only thing I ever thought about.
I said, "I'll have to get back to you on that."

After being examined by a specialist, the optometrist said,
"Your vision is fine, Mr. Dyson. Are you sure that you were having trouble with your eyes?"
I said, "What?!?"
He said, **"Are you sure you were having trouble with your eyes?"**
I said**, "What?!?"**

Don't participate in a lap dance,
while using your lap top.

I explained to my friend that I didn't talk to my uncle any more.
He said, "What does your uncle think of that?"
I said, "I don't know. I haven't told him yet."

I got in a fight with an arborist.
He tore me limb from limb!

I flunked out of coroner school.
I said, "He's dweed. He's dwed. He's deed."
The teacher said, "You just can't pronounce him dead, can you?"

Can you imagine if Diana Ross had been a policewoman?
"HALT, in the name of love, before you break my heart.
HALT, in the name..."

I think that Ben Bernanke is smoking marijuana.
He said that the economy is taking a hit.

I told my doctor that I had lost my health insurance.
He said, "You're cured!"

You can tell how old a kid is, if you ask him a specific TV question and he says,
"What Seventies Show?"

Admitting that he's gained a lot of weight,
Iggy Pop has changed his name to Biggy Pop.

You can tell that the mustard is too old when you can cut it.

People hear me and say, "You ought to be on the radio!"
Well, at one time, I **was** on the radio and the program director said,
"You out to be off the radio!"

They've recently found the original handwritten lyrics to the TV show theme song. It says, "Batman", followed by a bunch of ditto marks.

If this famous writer had ever been on the Jack Benny Show, would Jack have introduced him by saying, "Oh, Henry!"

I'm feeling kinda down today.
I took a CPR class... and my dummy died.

I have a theory as to why most men still have their left one.
Because the slogan isn't, "What would you **give** for a Klondike bar?"

A lot of people don't know that I went to Stanford.
I used to be a delivery truck driver. Went there all the time!

I found out the difference between typing and playing the piano.
Backspacing doesn't correct a mistake.

To improve my acting career,
I started taking performance enhancing drugs.

I tried out for a toilet paper commercial,
but I didn't get the roll.

I have a very talkative insurance agent.
Why, it took him almost an hour to save me 15 percent!

You know, kids are so different today.
Back when I was a kid, you'd never tell your parents what you thought of them....
right to their face!

You know, I just realized,
I've never been the star of a TV show that was canceled.

These two mailmen come walking into a bar, see.
One mailman says to the other mailman,
"Did your wife have the baby yet?"
The other mailman says, "Yes, I delivered it!"
The first mailman says, "How did you deliver it?"
The other mailman says, "Overnight!"

I see that they're adding a new category to Craig's List:
"Women seeking Craig"

On the road last night, a guy cut me off.
I've never seen such a long knife!

104

I tried to get the rooster to stop waking me up by saying,
"Cock a do do don't"

I've got one of those new, musical GPS units.
I asked it how to get to Art Garfunkel's house.
It said, "Take the long and winding road, bum bum...

When they play golf down in Mexico,
do they yell, "Quatro!"?

When I play golf, I can make a hole-in-one every time.
How come they fill those holes with water, anyway?

I found a way to hit my golf ball right beside the hole every time. I bring a shovel
with me.

You hear them say, "He's a strapping young man!",
but you never hear them say,
"She's a bra strapping young woman!"

Daryl Hall's singing partner had surgery today,
where the doctor was sewing his Oats.

Tom Bodet just opened a nudist camp.
His slogan is, "We'll leave nothing on for you"

A lot of people don't know that the original name of the singing group was.
"Frankie Valli and the Winter, Spring, Summer and Fall"

I tried to be a disk jockey once, but it just didn't work out. I was too sensitive:
I always cried when I announced, "That was 'Rainy Days and Mondays always get
me down' ... and now here's Bobby Goldsboro and 'Honey'...!"

Jobs may be slashed, as the Knife industry is facing cuts.
In a related story, sales of Band-Aids have soared.

I'm not a rubbernecker. There was a dresser on the freeway but I didn't look.
Now, if she was undressing, that would have been a different story.

After all these years, I finally got a flat tire.
Doing all those sit-ups really helped.

My book has made the Top Ten list.
Now, it's my tenth favorite book.

I own a Corinthian Leather jacket.

It's made out of a '78 Cordoba.

Citibank is using a Gene Pitney song in a new advertising campaign.
"It isn't very pretty what a town without Citi can do."

Barry Manalow has released a new album called, "Hits for People in their Eighties"

My uncle was having sexual problems.
He couldn't get the Viagra bottle open.

I was going to become a prison guard,
but I didn't want an inside job.

I wanted Terry Gross to review my book on NPR,
but she said that her show was called, "Fresh Air",
not "Hot Air".

I finally met my on-line girlfriend and found out that she not only stretched the truth,
she also has stretch marks.

When I said that I was looking for closure regarding my financial problems,
I didn't mean, **fore**closure.

I was hoping to buy a submarine,
but I couldn't get a subprime loan.

When I told my friend that I couldn't find my book on e-Bay, he clarified himself by saying,
"No, I saw it in the **East** Bay."

Sarah Palin has been asked to become the Ambassador to Russia.
"She'll be able to see her office from her house".

To stop the climb in the unemployment rate,
Donald Trump has been asked to stop firing people.

We could jump start the economy with a simple call to
Triple-A.

I was living on the fast track,
and then, the train came.

I wish that I could get my book on "America's Most Wanted".

I saw used copies of the Bible on Amazon.com with the tag line, "Only driven to church on Sundays".

If everybody loses their jobs,
the tax cuts WILL be permanent.

My Uncle refuses to take Viagra.
He won't put up with it.

I take medicine for the pain in my side,
primarily for the side effects.

The doctor said, "You don't stand up enough. Do you know what that means?"
I said, "I *under* stand".

After seeing my comedy act, the government accused me of being a suicide bomber.

An attorney advertises that he can help, even if you haven't paid taxes in years.
Apparently, he'll carry your bags into the cell for you.

The judge threw the book at OJ,
and he caught it for a ten-yard gain.

HP's top executive announced his retirement,
saying that he's out of toner.

I started carrying an identification card at a young age because my mother was
always yelling,
"Who do you think you are?"

I was real popular in grade school.
Everybody wanted to beat me up.

They found a sequel to Michael Jackson's "Billie Jean", using a song that goes like
this:
> "No sir, that's not my baby,
> Yes sir, I don't mean maybe,
> No sir, that's not my baby now."

When the employer found out that one of his employees died, he said, "So, Smith is
late again, huh?"

In court yesterday, they thought that I was someone else.
The clerk said, "Do you swear to tell the truth, the whole truth and nothing but the
truth...
so help you, God?"
I said, "Aaaaa, my name is Joe?"

My uncle was such a notorious liar that when he went to court, the clerk said,

"Do you swear to commit perjury, all perjury and nothing but perjury, so help you God?"
He said, "Aaaaa, no, of course not. Why would you think that?"

I was talking to my friend on the phone
and he said that he worked very hard to get where he is today.
I said, "Where are you?"
He said, "At work."

It's amazing how fast word gets around!
My doctor said to me, "Mr. Dyson, you don't have a chance."
At that very moment, I heard police megaphones saying,
"Come out, Mr. Dyson. You don't have a chance!"
I yelled, "I know!!!"
..... It's like, everybody knows before I do!!

My wife thinks that I have dementia.
She keeps saying, "Who do you think you are?"

I'm trying to get my dog a role on that TV show.
I'm teaching it how to play "The Walking Dead"

I didn't realize that after I learned the facts of life,
I had to learn the facts of wife.

Nowadays, everybody is using initials for everything:
lol, wtf, lmao.
Well, we used initials back in my day, too: LBJ, JFK, WWII.
We just capitalized them.

My father always told me: "Every time you get knocked down, get right back up!
And he was right. You can get run over lying in that parking lot!

My dog takes me too seriously.
Last night, I told him to play dead and he went into hospice.

Since Jerry Lewis is no longer the host of the Telethon,
he's tried out for another TV show. Here's what his audition sounded like:
"4, 3, 2, 1, Happy New Year, everyone!"

Do you know what tool they use to perform a Tummy Tuck?
A gut wrench.

Nobody ever took me seriously until I started doing standup comedy.

The North Korean President is learning how to speak English.
Then, he wants to threaten to drop the F Bomb.

When I'm shaving, I never play songs by Blood, Sweat and Tears.

They asked me why I always say, "We've been sitting on *them* all day."
I said that I always refer to my ass in the third person.

They asked me if I was going to go to church this week.
I said, "I don't know. What day is it?"

They asked me why I was only eating kurds.
I said because I lost my whey.

That football player, RG3 installed one of those automated phone answerers:
"To speak to RG1, press 1.... to speak to RG2, press 2, to speak to RG3, press 3..."

There was a freak accident at my house.
My wife broke her ankle bracelet.

They asked when we were going to get the bracelet fixed.
I said that the jewelry's out on that one.

I was prescribed schizophrenia medicine,
but I don't know which one of us should take it.

GM wants to build an electric vehicle that floats.
It will be called, The Chevy Boat.

I told my accountant that I couldn't get my car out of the driveway.
He told me to make a Reversing Entry.

I have a hard time believing my doctor.
He told me to cut down on sodium,
But I took it with a grain of salt.

My uncle was in court, charged with identity theft.
The court clerk said, "State your name, please".
He said, "Mine or the other guys?"

I can't believe the personal service that this company gave me.
They put my name right on the vacuum cleaner!

I went to the hardware store and I ordered a barrel.
The guy asked me what kind of barrel I wanted.
I said, "A wheel barrel."
Boy, it was a good thing he asked. Who knows what he would have brought me?

I've noticed that none of my on-line friends are fish.

The fish prefer to be my off-line friends

After watching Doctor OZ on TV, I gotta say,
that guy's got no brains, no heart and no courage.

Why don't they make a "4-hour Energy Drink".
I mean, they make a "5-Hour Energy Drink". Why not a "4-Hour Energy Drink"?
That way, you could drink
four, "5 Hour Energy Drinks" and
one, "4 Hour Energy Drink"
and stay up the whole 24 hours!

Tony Orlando saw my act and wrote a song about it.
"Tie a yellow ribbon around the old joke tree..."

When the girl down the street got pregnant, they made me take a DNA test.
Well, she had my D, and she had my N, but thank goodness she didn't have my A!

They asked me what I was doing to try to lose weight.
I said that I was taking blood thinners.

My personal budget is so bad that I'm thinking about becoming a non-profit.

They asked me where I had the operation.
I said that I left my prostate in San Francisco.

They asked me if I had a dental plan.
I said that I planned on getting one.

They asked me if I worried about being insured after I'm 65.
I said that I didn't medi-care.

My parents were so different.
My father would say, "I'm only going to say this, once....",
while my mother would say, "I'm only going to say this, over and over..."

In Australia, why doesn't water go up the drain?

I'm on a really tight budget.
The judge asked me if I was guilty or not guilty.
I said, "Which one is cheapest?"

I don't speak Spanish,
so when I drink beer,
I order Two-X's.

My mother used to give me answers in both English and Spanish.

110

If I asked for anything, she always said, "No"

You know what the most common injury reported is, at the Children's Hospital?
A boo boo. The second is an owie.

My Latin friend tries to learn English by repeating things that I say.
I said, "Do you see the sea?"
He said, "Si"

My uncle is so old that when he was a child,
St Joseph's aspirin was still being made by St Joseph.... himself.

I was ordering at the bar when some guy stepped in front of me and said,
"Give me a Bloody Mary"
I said, "Excuse me, it was my tourniquet."

You know, I never feel at home in a bar,
until I've been thrown through its plate glass window.

They asked me if I ever got a girl in trouble.
I said, "No. It was no trouble at all."

I misunderstood my doctor.
I called him up after Obama was elected and he said,
"No, Joe. I didn't say to call me up, four hours after the Election"

Before going to the beach, I asked the hippie what the tide was like.
He said, "It was high, man!"

So many men are suffering from sexual performance problems,
that I saw a note on the bathroom wall that said,
"For a bad time, call Charlie at 271-12......"

When a nudist takes a shower, is he doing the laundry?

They asked me if my car was a limousine.
I said, "That's a stretch."

They're going to make a new spy thriller about James Bond's cat.
It's called "You Only Live Nine Times"

I said to my friend, "I notice that your car has new hub caps."
He said, "They're not hub caps. They're wheel covers."
I said, "Why did you get new wheel covers?"
He said, "Because somebody stole my hub caps!"

I'm sorry that I'm late.

I had to take my cat to the Flea Market.

I told my wife that she was a real dish,
so she threw herself at me.

They asked me if I believed in natural child birth.
I said, "Naturally"

After the surgery, they said that my voice would be a little horse. And they were right!
When I woke up, the first thing I said was, "Hello, I'm Mr. Ed"

At work, they have a First Aid Kit with a sign that says,
"Only use after breaking glass"

I found out something about my favorite beer, today.
It's also drunk by The Most *Uninteresting* Man in the world.

They asked me why I never had kids.
I said, "Because I didn't want to have to say,
'Son, you've got some pretty small shoes to fill.'"

I got kicked out of pilot school.
They said that I had a bad altitude.

The cop asked me why I drove past the DUI check point.
I said that I had trouble stopping under the influence.

I was at the Home Depot and I couldn't control myself.
I got into one of those vehicles that goes "Beep, beep, beep, beep" and drove it around.
Wouldn't you know it. They charged me with Forklifting.

I called a company and the operator said, "Hello, this is Hans."
I said, "Hello, Hans, I need to return an item."
He said, "I'll have to transfer you. This is out of my Hans."

Do you remember the commercial that the Bee Gees made?
"How do you mend the heartbreak of psoriasis?"

You can lose a lot of weight in prison.
I hear that OJ has lost almost 4 gallons.
…. Lost 4 gallons of OJ

Everybody thought that Thomas Edison was crazy.
Before his invention, people would describe him by saying,
"The candle is lit but nobody's home."

I'll always remember the day that Eli Whitney walked into the bar and said,
"I've invented the Cotton Gin."

Thanksgiving, **1776**, they asked our first president to cut the turkey.
He said, "Who do I look like? George Washington **Carver**?"

They said that Abraham Lincoln had trouble making up his mind.
"Four score and six or seven years ago…. Actually, it might have been three scores
ago…
Or was it four?"

The doctor told me to take my medications, religiously.
So I take them every Sunday.

When the judge asked the defendant why he committed his third strike,
He said that he had lost count.

I just realized something:
If I lose my will to live, I'll *find* my will to *die.*

I don't know what they teach the kids today about musical history.
I was talking to a bunch of kids, and they think that **The Carpenters** built stuff.

Another kid asked me what the Grateful Dead were called back when they were
alive.

My dog's so gullible.
He thinks that I have a Master's degree.

My Dad was notorious for stopping at the bar every night.
In fact, if I was bad, my mother would say,
"You just wait until your Father doesn't come home!"

I knew that my trial was in jeopardy when my own attorney jumped up and yelled,
"He did it! And he's glad he did it! And he'd do it again! Do you hear me? He'd do it
again!"

I just saw a performance of "To Kill a Mockingbird", starring my cat.

My ears are always lying to me.
I can't believe my ears!

Let's play "To Tell The Truth". See if you can determine which of these men is
telling the truth:
"My name is Clark Kent."
"My name is Clark Kent."

"My name is Super...aaaa... Clark Kent."

Now that my hair has turned salt and pepper,
I'm a man for all seasonings.

A young person asked me why I pull my pants up all the way.
I said, "So I have something to do when I go to the bathroom"

Even politicians are wearing their pants pulled down.
Yesterday I saw Barbara's Boxer's.

Defending himself against charges of infidelity, my uncle said,
"It was only a 'thank-you' kiss."
My aunt said, "It lasted for an hour and a half! What do you say to that?"
He said, "You're welcome!"

Do you know what I hate about bald guys?
They never get old!

Nobody ever calls them, "Whitey"

I told the man that I was a bean counter.
He asked how long I had been doing that.
I said, "For seven beans, now."
(...or was it six beans?)

My friend is always talking to himself.
Every time I try to say something, he says, "Hey, don't interrupt me!"

If you can only fit two people in the front of a moving van,
Where do they put the other five Santini Brothers?

They asked me if there was any country where I couldn't find anything to drink.
I said that I was thirsty in Hungary.

The cop asked me why I was speeding.
I said that I was using Rapid Transit.

If you're trying to get a new insurance policy from Geico,
Don't call them at fourteen minutes till five.

I asked the guy how he knew that I was going, "Dat Dat, Dat Dat Dat, Dat Dat"
He said that I was telegraphing it.

They're going to remake an old TV show using a rock star.
It will be called, "The Courtship of Iggy's Pop"

They're advertising a new, natural way to learn a new language where you're taught the same way that you learned your first language.
Apparently, they teach the language to your mother, first, and then she teaches you.

I've discovered that Samuel Adams was the first pioneer to be charged with Riding under the Influence.

Other names considered by Hank Ketchum for his comic strip:
Lincoln the Delinquent
Brooke the Crook
Leif the Thief

My fairy godmother said, "What would you give to have everything you've always wanted?"
I said that I'd give everything!
Boy, that didn't last long!

If somebody ever steals my identity,
I hope they do it, right after I've been convicted of murder.

Ever since the laser eye surgery,
My printer sees much better.

The doctor said that I could stand to lose some weight.
I stood up, and didn't lose an ounce!

None of Lincoln's original writings were sold at a recent auction.
Bidders claimed that the writings weren't worth the shovel they were written on.

I heard that Slim Whitman passed away.
Slim was ninety when he died…. Which was slim for Slim.

I thought that my uncle was hungry and thirsty,
Instead, he was in Hungary on Thursday.

To get more people to sign up for Classmates.com, they've added a new question to the application:
"Which High School did you drop out of?"

After talking to a suicide hot line, Patrick Henry said,
"Give me liberty."

The judge told me that it was illegal for a 14 year old to have sex with an adult.
I said, "Go easy on her, Judge. I'm sure she didn't know."

I'm always the last to hear everything.
I didn't know that I was getting laid off until my goodbye party.

My uncle realized that he might be getting divorced when he was in Yahoo and saw his face among, "Singles in Your Area"

Lassie, describing her career: "First, Jeff fell in the well, then Timmy fell in the well, then Ranger Corey Stewart fell in the well...."

I came out of the closet yesterday.
It happened right after the cop yelled, "Come out with your hands up!"

I bought this house, specifically because they said that it had an Ocean view.
I opened the curtain and all I could see was my neighbor!
Come to find out, he's Billy Ocean.

If he sings Caribbean Queen, one more time.....

You know, we'd be in a lot of trouble if Don McLean had written his song... just a little differently...
"I drove my Civic to the Pacific...
and the Pacific was dry...."

At one time, I hit my head and lost my memory for a while.
I couldn't remember anything....
except where my glasses were and where my keys were...

After being charged with shooting his two-timing wife and her boyfriend,
he told the judge that it was a hunting accident.
He was hunting Love Birds.

They asked me why I only go to the New Year's Party and the Christmas Party.
I said because I believe in the two-party system.

I found out how Dennis the Menace got his nickname.
The first time that he was arrested, the police chief said,
"That's Mitchell's kid. You know, Mitchell the Menace."

The judge tried to charge me with Forgery.
I said, "That's ridiculous! I drive a Dodgery!"

They asked me what kind of sewing machines they use in the Federal Prisons.
I said, "Sing Singers"

The cop said, "My police dog is barking. He thinks you have drugs on you."
I said, "Look, now he's licking his butt. Does he think I have hemorrhoids, too?"

They asked me how I got my hair to stand up.
I said that I've been using Scott's Anti-Gravity.

Tests of the new solar electric chair aren't going so well,
since they execute people at midnight.

I thought that I saw Phil Mickelson.
I said to some guy, "Hey, is that Lefty?"
He said, "That's righty."
I said, "Oh, I thought it was Lefty."

They asked me why I paid my housecleaner in 60 second intervals.
I said because she's a Minute Maid

You know where the worst fishing in the world is?
The Dead Sea

Every time my life insurance agent calls up, he starts the conversation by saying,
"Is Mr. Dyson still alive?"

One of the most dangerous jobs is being a Court Recorder.
For example, the judge asked the Court Recorder to read back the testimony:
"I did it, and I'm glad I did it, and I'd do it again. Do you hear me? I'd do it again."
The judge said, "Bailiff, take the court recorder into custody!"

I tried to do some cow tipping,
but I didn't know what percentage to leave.

I have an answer to the question, "How do you mend a broken heart?"
Cure psoriasis!

I didn't know if the surgery was going to do me any good.... at this age,
and sure enough, I've come back... good as old.

I was reading the side of a prescription bottle of this expensive drug that I take and
it said, "Do not take this drug if you are pregnant."
Great! Now I have to pay for a pregnancy test!

After hearing my jokes, the government decided to stop listening to my phone calls.

I got Simply Red to write a song about my act.
"Holding back the laughs......"

I avoid clinical depression.
I stay out of the clinic.

Almost immediately, the makers of that program,
"Go To Meeting" realized their mistake.
They quickly released a new program called,

"Come *Back* From Meeting"

You know, I keep getting mistaken for Bert Reynolds... which isn't good news.
Have you seen how old he is now?

The coach asked me if I had any muscles.
I said that muscles weren't my strong point.

The Phys Ed teacher said that I should see a conditioning coach.
I said, "In *my* condition?"

I got stopped at a DUI check point where the cop asked me how many fingers he
was holding up.
I said, "Officer, is this a drunk test or a math test?"

After giving me a physical, the doctor asked me if I had any other problems.
I said, "Yes, I hurt my knee."
He said, "When did that happen?"
I said, "About ten minutes ago when you hit it with that little hammer."

There's been a breakup in my household.
I lost my Coffee Mate.

I told my doctor that I couldn't sleep longer than sixty minutes at a time.
He asked, "How often does this happen?"
I said, "Every waking hour."

A lot of people who came over on the Nina, the Pinta and the Santa Maria were
disappointed when they got here.
They thought they were going to the *Nude* World.

You know, a lot of people think that I'm the savior.
I'll walk into a crowded room and everybody will say, "Oh my God!!!"

It's amazing how starting your own business can change your attitude.
Before he started his famous "List", Craig was listless.

After his doctor's appointment, my uncle said, "I'm going to the Great Beyond"
I said, "Well that's just great! I have no vacation time and *you're* going to the Great
Beyond!"

My mother always knew when I wanted something, ahead of time.
She was always saying, "You're asking for it!"

I was the oldest kid in my 12th grade class.
I had a senior moment.

Adam was the first member of a sports team
He would stand in the field and yell, "I'm Number One! I'm Number One!"

I found out something about Police Dogs.
"Sit" and "Lay down" don't work with them.

They asked me if I ever did open Mikes.
I said that Mike was open to it, but I wasn't.

Times sure are changing.
I met a girl who said that she was into 'pre-living together' sex.

I was so surprised when I heard that Elvis had recorded song called "Jailhouse Rock".
I didn't know that he had a prison record.

They asked me if I cared that so many inventions we heard about growing up, never came to be.
I said, "I couldn't give a flying car."

My company is so far behind on its paperwork,
I was just named, "Employee of Last Month"

When my friends said that they had gone to one bar after another without me,
I was bar hopping mad!

They introduced me to a basketball player that was so tall,
I had to shake his leg.

They say that Aretha Franklin didn't write the song, "Respect",
even though she could spell it.

They asked me if I wanted a hamburger patty.
I said that I'd take Patty without the hamburger.

I told my wife that I didn't feel very well.
She told me to take off the gloves.
She was right. I feel much better now.

I could tell that my car was near the end when it started stuttering:
"Da da da da da dat's all, folks"

When I got married and they said, "…until death do you part,"
I said, "This is a wife or death situation"

They say that "Love means never having to say you're sorry",
But some flowers and a box of candy sure help.

After failing a lie detector test,
Barry Manalow recorded a new song:
"I didn't write the songs that makes whole world sing…"

I tried to get one of those payday loans,
But nobody would lend me their payday.

How come we say redundant things, like mail man?
Why don't we just say, "Here comes the Mail", or "Here comes the Man"?

After telling me about his huge personal lose,
I said to my friend, "So, how are you doing?"
He said, "I'm taking it, one day at a time."
I said, "Oh no! You're not drinking again, too, are ya?"

The Sixties rock group, The Association are reuniting and putting out a new album
based on what they've learned in life.
The new songs are:
"Cherish May Not Be the Word",
"Never say Never, My Love",
"At this Point, Everyone has known Windy", and
"Along Comes Mary with Her Walker"

My Father would have loved it if I wore my pants like the kids do now.
It would have saved him a step when he spanked me.

The doctor asked me why I was being affected by second hand smoke.
I said, "Because I hold my coffee cup in my first hand.

My uncle was so broke when he died that he was funeral homeless.

They asked me if I ever got a letter in high school sports.
I said, "Sure. It was an 'F'"

My boss said that I was being transferred to our satellite office.
I said, "When do I leave?"
He said, "10, 9, 8, 7, 6…."

I asked the repairman to fix my watch.
He said, "When did it stop working?"
Looking at my wrist, I said, "Ten-thirty."

The cops surrounded me and yelled, "Drop your weapon!"
So, I dropped my joke book!

I used to be a schizophrenic comedian.

I'd open my act by saying, "Both of us come walking into a bar, see..."

If you're going to be a name dropper,
don't drop Humpty Dumpty.

I found out, after you do some money laundering,
don't iron it.

They said that I was taking comedy too seriously.
I said, "Yeah, me and my audience."

After waiting for 43 years, The Three Dog Night released a new song.
"Eli's not coming"

If you're in a car right now, you're very close to a Geico commercial.

In Great Britain, the Monarch is the star of that TV show, "Queen for Twenty-Two
Thousand Days"

I found out something yesterday.
Don't ride your bike through a car wash.
For some reason, I thought those brushes would feel good.

I go to the dumbest vet.
I called him up and said that my cat was throwing up wads of fur.
He said, "Sounds like she has hair balls."
I said, "Doc! She's a female cat! How can she have hair balls?
(What do they teach these guys?)

I updated my Linked In profile to include standup comedy.
Now, I keep having friends, UnEndorse me.

I asked the doctor if he was going to x-ray me.
He said, "Only if you don't take your clothes off."

My uncle is committed to everything he does.
Why, just yesterday, he committed adultery.

If you can't use the Lord's name in vain,
how do you swear to God?

How come your car doesn't have a "Don't Check Engine" light?

I was terrible at math.
I can't count how many "F"s I got.

The judge asked me, "Have you ever served on a jury?"

I said, "Yes, we sentenced him to death."
The judge said, "So, it was a murder trial."
I said, "No, the guy aggravated us so much that we decided to kill him."

As I got older, people said that I wasn't acting as cool or far out as I used to,
so I got a Hippie replacement.

In my neighborhood, the garbage man will pick up yard debris.
I wanted to make friends with my garbage man, so I tossed him an olive branch.

When my uncle got sick, the doctor asked me, "Are you going to care for your
loved one?"
I said that I hate my uncle.
He said, "In that case, are you going to care for your hated one?"

The transplant doctor told me that my new heart was coming on a ship.
But then, the ship sank.
When I heard that, my heart sank!

On the radio, that commentator, Charles Osgood read a commercial about Identity
Theft.
He finished the spot by saying, "To get a discount, use my name, "Osgood".
So I called up the company and said, "Hello, this is Charles Osgood...."

I found the cheapest insurance company.
It's called, "NoState"
"You're in no hands with NoState"

Oh, I found out, Don't reserve Room 7 at Motel 6

Every time Ben Bernanke would talk about the economy, I'd say, "Oh, Brother!"
Now, they've replaced him with a woman. "Oh, Sister!"

They told me that my name tag was upside down.
I looked down and said, "No, it isn't."

After finding rolling papers in the house, my wife said, "Have you been smoking
catnip again?"
I said, "Meow! Meow! Meow!"

I answered the phone and the voice said, "May I speak to the woman of the house?"
I said, "Who's calling, please?"
He said, "The man of the phone."

My doctor recommended that I take aspirin.
I said that I'd like nine out ten opinions on that.

My wife asked me to paint the house.
I said, "What makes you think that I can paint a house?"
She said, "Well, you paint the town every night!"

I hate waiting for plumbers,
so I called the guy who advertised himself as the Punctual Plumber
He showed up 3 hours late!
I said, "Hey! I thought you were the Punctual Plumber!"
He handed me an apology note that had perfect punctuation.

I'm glad that they don't sell ducks at the Dollar Store.
They'd be a buck a duck.

You hear a lot about that singer, Jay Z,
but you never hear about his brother, Lay...
Lay Z.

When they told me that I had been defeated, I said, "Good gracious!"
I was gracious in defeat.

I misunderstood my publisher.
I thought he said that people wanted a Kindle version of my book.
Instead, he said that people wanted to use my book as kindling.

It's not too bad living in a high crime neighborhood during the winter.
The gun fire keeps me warm.

I'm not as quick as I used to be.
In fact, it's so bad that I have to drink Nestlé's Slow.

My aunt was a horrible waitress.
She wouldn't take orders from anyone!

My wife said that she couldn't live without me.
I said, "Did the doctor tell you that?"

The quickest way to go to sleep, is to stand up to a bully.

Every insurance company except one have merged together.
The new insurance company will be called, "Not Geico"

I have to work between 5 and 7 o'clock in the evening,
so I can only go to the bar during "Un-Happy Hour".

More Rock Star News:
The members of 3-Dog Night admitted that they were abused as puppies.

My job requires me to travel quite a bit.
The rest room is over in the other building.

As a child, my father could never spank me when we were boating.
We were always up a creek without a paddle.

On the way to a company picnic, the bus rolled over, killing all of the Insurance agents.
The Insurance Company was quickly sued for their advertising slogan, "Live agents are standing by."

Due to prison overcrowding, they have to use every empty room.
My uncle was sentenced to Life in the Gas Chamber.

I have some advice for you.
Don't try to get change for a dollar at the 99 cent store.

The cop said that he was charging me with Road Rage.
I said, "WHAT?!!!"

I accidently parked my car in the tow-away zone,
so they towed my car away.
I called the police and said, "I'd like to report a towlin car."

I got turned down by Geico for an insurance policy because,
it took me longer than 15 minutes to describe all the accidents I had been in.

They asked me how I got paint on my fingers.
I said it was from hanging those "Wet Paint" signs.

The doctor said that I should give up drinking.
I said, "You first!"
He said, "Well, maybe you should give up smoking instead"

I have a tip about trying to save money on toilet paper.
Don't try Charmin Lite.

Statistics say that one out of every four persons is suffering from some sort of mental illness.
That's crazy! That's just crazy!

I went to a car auction and bought one of those old police interceptors.
You should see the look on those cop's faces when you intercept one.

I hear that legendary Chuck Norris wants to become a professional baseball player.
He was signed by the Texas Rangers.

My agent is getting me a try out for a new TV series.
It's called, "Two Woman and a Half a Man"

Every time I told the girl that I wanted to get to first base with her, she'd throw me out.

They asked me if my father ever played paddle ball with me.
I said, "Thank goodness, no! He always paddled my butt."

When I was little, Billy Joel was invited to speak at my Sunday School class.
When I got home, my Mother asked me what I had learned in church that day.
I said that Catholic girls start much too late.

The little kid asked me if I remembered the 20th Century.
I said, "Son, I even remember the Buick Century!"

I'm looking forward taking a Carnival cruise.
I can't wait to ride the Ferris wheel!

I just found out that the high beam switch isn't on the floorboard anymore.
I wondered why the car speeded up every time I put on the brights!

My friend said, "Look at all this stuff I stole!"
I said, "You're joking!"
He said, "No, I took it seriously!"

The company said that I was working an "at will" job.
I said, "Where will I be working?"
They said, "At Will's house."

Last night, I was at the bar for the Last Call.
The bartender covered the receiver and said,
"Hey, Dyson! It's your wife. She says she's leaving you!"
It was the last call.

The Pope has announced a new policy for the church. It's called, "Don't ask, don't tell during confession."

I said, "Doc, I have a frog in my throat. What's the worst that can happen to me?"
He said, "You'll croak."

I met the girl of my dreams once.
I asked her out and she said, "You must be dreaming."

The cop asked me, "Have you been drinking?"
I said that I haven't had a drink since 1968.
He said, "What year is it?"

I said, "1968!"

Billy Joel is updating one of his songs to include the Gay population.
The song now says, "Catholic **boys** start much too late."

It's tough getting old. I was looking at a beautiful young lady when my friend said,
"Hey, that girl's young enough to be your daughter's daughter's daughter."

With the recession, I've been sacrificing.
I only eat sacrificial lamb.

The girl said, "I never want to see you again!"
I said, "Good! Next time, we'll leave the lights off."

The city set up a special day where you could turn in outdated drugs.
So I turned in some purple haze. Nobody's doing purple haze anymore. It's outdated.

My parents thought I was deaf.
They were always yelling at me.

Tommy and Dickie are coming back to TV. The new sitcom will be called:
"How I Met Your Smothers"

If you're having trouble with ED,
don't go to a shrink.

It's tough getting old. I was looking at an older woman when my friend said,
"Hey, that woman's old enough to be your daughter."

The marriage counselor said that I should be more open in my marriage.
I said that my wife was against having an open marriage.

The best way to handle a carjacker is to sing to him:
"Hit the road, carjacker, and don't you come back no more, no more, no more, no
more..."

When I picked up my date, she said, "Is that a snake in your pocket or are you just
happy to see me?"
I said, "AAAAAAAAAAAAAH! It's a snake!!!!"

A tree fell in my yard last night, just missing my dog.
Thank goodness, he was barking up the wrong tree.

When they cancelled my swimming lesson, my heart sunk!

I saw a kid who was wearing his pants pulled down so far,
that his knees buckled..... because that's where the buckle was.

126

I can't believe the prices at the barber shop, nowadays.
I said, "How much for a shave and a haircut"
He said, "Eighty bits."

Yesterday, I got run off the road.
As the guy drove past me, he yelled,
"Stop running on the road!"

I found out, they don't let you yell bad words on the basketball court.
I foul-languaged out.

I said, "How much for a fortune cookie?"
He said, "Ten bucks."
I said, "Ten dollars! That's a fortune!"
"Well, how much would you expect to pay for a fortune cookie?"

The cop asked me how fast I was going.
I said, "Godspeed!"

Last night, I was finally in a bar fight where I **didn't** get thrown through the plate glass window.
It was made of Plexiglas.

The girl at the bar said to me, "Why do I get the feeling that you're married?"
My wife said, "It's probably the wedding ring."

My wife called me at the bar and asked if I could find somebody to be a designated driver.
I called out, "Hey! Does anybody here know how to ride a bike?"

My uncle got a heart transplant.
Come to find out, they got the heart from a guy who was heartbroken!
Now, all my uncle does is sit around and think about that guy's old girl friend.

Legendary Dion Warwick songs are being released, updated for a lady her age.
Songs include:
"Walk your Walker on By"
"Do you know the way to..., to, to..."
"Say a lot of prayers for you"
"What the world needed then"

I went with the security guards because I thought they wanted me to throw out the first ball.
Instead, they wanted to throw *me* out first.

The doctor asked me to rate my sex life on a scale of 1 to 10.

I said, "10 would be the most amount of pain, right?"

When I saw a friend of mine at the ball park,
I started doing The Wave.

They found a typo in the police handbook, which is apparently causing criminals to escape.
The handbook says, "Ready, Don't Aim, Fire!"

My uncle can't remember anything.
You always have to remind him.
Like in court yesterday, the judge was always reminding him that he was under oath.

My financial situation is so sick,
I have to take my books to the doctor.
.... to get them doctored....

A football player has been slapped with a paternity suit.
It was filed by RG4.

The lady said that she was 36-24-36.
I said, "That's what I figured."

If a vegetarian runs over a tomato,
is that road kill?

My wife and I were having an argument
She said, "You never take out that garbage."
I said, "That's rubbish!"
She said, "Okay, you never take out the rubbish!"

I'm learning a new language.
They're teaching me how to talk to my cat.
Here's what I've learned so far:
"Meow, Esavelle. Como esta?
Estoy bein gracious, meow?"

My brother was always making telling statements.
He'd say, "I'm telling Mom!"

It hurts to get hair implants.
Then I found out - "Rogaine - No Pain"

Boy, did I get ripped off!
I bought a can of evaporated milk.
I opened it and it was filled with evaporated water!

128

The doctor told me that my leg injury would disable me for about 6 weeks.
I said, "Does that mean that I can park in that special space in front of your office?"
He said, "Actually, yes."
I said, "Hang on a minute, Doc. Let me go move my car."

My wife only likes to argue with **me**,
so when we get in the car together, I turn off Rush Limbaugh.

When I was young, I remember having to ask my Dad about sex.
Now, I have to ask him about erectile dysfunction.

I have a tip for all you guys.
The best way to stop from throwing out your back is:
Don't pick up any girls.

They found a warehouse full of chemical weapons yesterday.
It was filled with cans of "Raid Ant and Insurgent Killer."

When the new nurse came on duty, she said,
"Mr. Dyson? Joe? How would you like to be referred to?"
I said, "Just call me what the other nurses do."
She said, "Okay, asshole. How are you doing this morning?"

I yelled to the cop, "Hey! That guy's trying to kill me!"
He said, "Well, you *are* in the gas chamber, Mr. Dyson"

I'm against gun control!
I mean, what if my horse breaks its leg?

There's going to be a new Jackie Chan movie.
In this one, he plays a convict in a foreign prison.
It's called, "Sing Sing Singapore"

While admitting me to the hospital, they said,
"Do you have any religious preference?"
I said, "That depends on my diagnosis."

Madonna announced that she's ending her, "Like a Virgin" tour.
Ya think?

Folks, I'd like to step out of character for a moment and answer a question that I'm often asked?
Where do the jokes in this book come from?
Well, I have a computer, and a program called Microsoft Word.
I type the jokes on the screen and print them on this special machine.
It's called a printer.
So I hope that answers your question, "Where do the jokes in this book come from?"

Hey folks, if you haven't read, "**You and I are Intertwined** yet", put it on your list. It's the funniest book of the year!

Joe Dyson

Write to me at **Jdys74@Yahoo.com**
Other books by Joe Dyson
"Never Entertain During Watermelon Season"
"One Year of One Liners"

Made in the USA
San Bernardino, CA
08 March 2015